LANCASTER
AT WAR 4

LANCASTER
AT WAR 4:
Pathfinder Squadron

Alex Thorne

LONDON
IAN ALLAN LTD

Contents

Published by Ian Allan Ltd, Shepperton, Surrey; and printed by Ian Allan Printing Ltd at their works at Coombelands in Runnymede, England

Editor's Note

Readers will notice that the author of this book and the captain of the crew whose exploits are related herein are one and the same person. At the author's request, the story is related in the third person.

Photographs have been carefully selected to illustrate as clearly as possible life on an operational training unit and Pathfinder squadron. Readers will appreciate that, for obvious reasons, it is impossible to find a photograph of each individual aircraft and person described; the majority of photographs are, therefore, representative of the aircraft, persons, procedures and actions described in the text.

Acknowledgements

The author wishes to thank the following individuals and organisations for their assistance in the preparation of this book: Chaz Bowyer for his invaluable help with caption research and the provision of illustrations; the Public Record Office, Kew, Richmond, Surrey; the Imperial War Museum, London, for kind permission to photograph the inside of Lancaster DV372 in the museum's collection, members of his crew and other wartime colleagues such as Jimmy Hughes and Jack Catford, former rear gunners in the Pathfinder Force, who so often reminded him of events and technical details which he had forgotton in the passage of time; and thanks particularly to his friends Pat and Tony Ryan for their invaluable help over many months in transferring his tape-recorded text on to their word processor.

Previous page:
Lancaster PA238 SR-Z of No 101 Squadron gets airborne at Poningliano in 1945.
Via A. S. Thomas

All uncredited photographs are from the Chaz Bowyer collection.

Introduction

It was well past breakfast time on the morning of 28 July 1944 when the crew of Lancaster D-Dog No 635 (Pathfinder) Squadron, were awakened by the airman who looked after their sleeping quarters — one of a dozen huts in the orchard of the vicarage behind the XIIth century church in the village of Bexwell, within a stone's throw of the Bomber Command airfield near Downham Market, in Norfolk.

Twelve hours earlier they had been at 19,000ft over Hamburg on their first operation. The post-operation reports had been completed, D-Dog was secure on its dispersal, and as the crew trudged wearily along the country lane leading from the airfield to their quarters there was one thought in all their minds: will we be on again tomorrow? It was a question they would ask themselves many times until they landed their Lancaster for the last time on 18 April the following year, after leading a daylight raid on Heligoland.

This volume of *Lancaster at War* describes the crew's participation in four widely differing operations. It might also provide new insights into what life was like on a Pathfinder station, the organisation and techniques which were a turning point in the effectiveness of Bomber Command, and the comradeship of its crews which exists to this day among those who are still with us.

Alex Thorne
Surrey 1989

Right:
HM King George VI making a not infrequent visit to a Lancaster Squadron.
Crown Copyright

ACM Sir Arthur Harris became AOC-in-C,
Bomber Command on 22 February 1942 until
14 September 1945. Known affectionately, if
pragmatically, as 'Butch' to all bomber crews,
Harris later became Marshal of the RAF and
died on 5 April 1984, a few days before his

1
Blind Faith and a Lot of Hope

THE truth in the age-old maxim that a chain is only as strong as its weakest link was continuously demonstrated in Bomber Command during the early years of World War 2.

In June 1940 the fall of France brought to a sudden and dramatic end the months of so-called 'phoney war'. It was the prelude to the terror raids in which a large part of London was destroyed. High explosive and incendiary bombs also fell on provincial targets which included Bristol, Portsmouth, Plymouth and Coventry. It was purely destructive non-selective area bombing and it did a tremendous amount of damage. The result was to harden the British spirit: the will to fight was not affected, but the means to fight were. A lot of production capacity was lost in those raids which was the signal for a big effort both by Bomber Command and the aircraft industry to make the Command more effective. But when we replied by attacking enemy targets by night — until then most of our 'bombs' had been pamphlets — our aircraft were equipped with a compass, airspeed indicator, altimeter, and a lot of blind faith.

The results were negligible. Our bombers flew over a blacked-out Germany through searchlight belts, subject to heavy fire from the ground and attacks from enemy fighters. Many of the bombs fell on dummy targets. The Command's losses were heavy and the operations were almost a complete failure. Unfortunately, the weak point was too often located at the top of the chain of command. From the first day when a lone Blenheim took off from Wyton on a reconnaissance flight over Wilhelmshaven there followed a stream of constantly changing directives from the Air Ministry to Bomber Command. A plethora of politicians, scientists, and professors of various denominations, as well as 'experts' in bombing strategy and tactics, bombarded the Air Ministry with conflicting advice and criticism. Constantly changing priority targets were announced and in whatever happened to come out as the strategy of the month, or day, the aircrews at the end of the chain of command paid a high price. Winston Churchill, the Prime Minister, paid tribute to them in his famous 'never in the field of human

ACM Sir Edgar Ludlow Hewitt was AOC-in-C, Bomber Command from 12 September 1937 to 2 April 1940.

conflict' speech in Parliament on 20 August 1940. '. . . they plod steadily on, taking their aircraft through fair weather and foul, night after night and sometimes by day.'

The results of their press-on spirit were, unhappily, not commensurate with their efforts. How could they have been, without the backing from a chain of command capable of presenting from the top a unanimity in purpose and planning? In the two-and-a-half years following the outbreak of war there had been three Commanders-in-Chief of Bomber Command — Air Marshals Sir Edgar Ludlow-Hewitt, Sir Charles (later Lord) Portal, and Sir Richard Peirse. But the arguments at the top continued — until February 1942 when Air Marshal Sir Arthur Harris took over as C-in-C. As a former Commander of No 5 Group, Harris had never hesitated to say what he thought of the directives and counter-directives with which the Group Commanders had to contend. In reply to one of them he is reported as having replied to the Deputy Chief of Air Staff: 'In your last directive you failed to indicate the precise moment at which my pilots

should blow their noses.' It was the start of a new era for Bomber Command when he arrived at its headquarters in High Wycombe, and it was to continue until victory was achieved three years and three months later.

One of the new C-in-C's first actions was to establish a chain of command with interdependent links. Every morning the leaders of all his operational sections would assemble in the operations room at HQ. They always included his target advisor and the officers responsible for intelligence, meteorology, navigation, radio and radar, armaments and engineering. When they had decided on the target they would work out the number of aircraft to be used, having regard to the daily reports on the numbers available from each Group in the Command. Their decisions were then transmitted to the selected Groups which then decided on the squadrons and the number of aircraft to be provided by each of them. The chain of actions would continue through the squadron commanders who would select their crews and brief the section leaders on their respective responsibilities. Everything had to be completed within a matter of hours and there were many other vital details to be arranged. In fact, there would be few members of a squadron who would not be directly involved, from the WAAF teams who drove the crews to their aircraft, the airmen and airwomen in the parachute sections, and the catering personnel who had to be prepared to produce meals at any specified hours, the medical staff, flying control, police and, of course, ground staff who would be working on the aircraft at their dispersals, possibly in most unpleasant weather conditions.

It was hard going for everybody in the first year of the Harris regime. He was convinced that the quickest way to victory was to concentrate his forces on targets in Germany, and not to be at the beck and call of other Services as was so often demanded. Eventually he got his way and in April 1943 the Air Ministry agreed: 'Bomber Command should revert as far as possible to attacks on targets in Germany'. That was just eight months after another development which was to have a significant effect on the bomber offensive.

A New Force in Bomber Command

In Canada, at the beginning of the war, there was a young man in charge of operations on the Atlantic Ferry. During the winter of 1940/41 he was called to the Air Ministry in London several times to discuss the problem of why our aircrews were failing to find their targets. His name was Don Bennett and he asked the officers at the Ministry if they could climb into an ill-equipped bomber and fly hundreds of miles to find a pinpoint target in the darkness despite all the dummies and spoofs, the lack of dependable met information and all the other problems. Something, he suggested, had to be done — and quickly.

So the idea of a Pathfinder Force was conceived. It would bring together selected airmen of Bomber Command and its task would be to identify the target, mark it with specially developed flares, and then control the attack of the main bomber force. The principle was accepted by the War Cabinet and the idea was pressed on Bomber Command. The C-in-C at that time, Air Marshal Sir Richard Peirse, refused to have anything to do with it, and

Above:
The Avro Lancaster first entered service with No 44 Squadron at Waddington in late December 1941, and flew its first operations on 10/12 March 1942. Here Lancaster F-Freddie of No 83 Squadron at Scampton is seen overflying the English countryside.

in due course he was succeeded by Air Marshal Sir Arthur Harris.

Between the wars, Bennett served with the Royal Australian Air Force, and in 1931 he transferred to the Royal Air Force. Three years later he joined Imperial Airways, and in 1938 he made the first commercial crossing of the North Atlantic in *Mercury*, the upper component of the *Mayo* composite aircraft. He was co-founder of the Atlantic Ferry Command and was re-commissioned into the RAF in 1941 as a wing commander in command of No 77 Squadron. When leading an attack on the German battleship *Tirpitz* he was shot down but escaped to Sweden, returning to the UK to command No 10 Squadron. The following year he formed the Pathfinder Force.

Sadly, Air Vice-Marshal Don Bennett CB, CBE, DSO died from a heart attack in September 1987 only a few weeks before he would have officially opened the Pathfinder Corner in the Bomber Command Museum at Hendon. Some years before he died he had given the author of this book the transcript of a paper he had read to the Royal Aeronautical Society Historical Group. The following extracts convey a first-hand description of the formation, organisation and tactics of the Pathfinder Force.

The Don Bennett Story

" 'Bert' Harris achieved one resounding success soon after he took over at Bomber Command. He laid on the first 1,000-bomber raid against Cologne to show what could be done. Its purpose, no more and no less, was to save the Command's offensive. The War Cabinet was tired of the failure of this, our only real means of aggression, and they were on the point of wrapping it up. So Harris brought out all the aircraft and crews he could muster. The only one he did not get was me, because I returned only that night from Norway after being shot down a month previously. Harris then tried two more 1,000-bomber raids, both on the Ruhr, but neither of them was successful. The War Cabinet's anxiety was renewed and they finally insisted that a Pathfinder Force be tried.

" 'Bert' Harris opposed it at first for several reasons, the main one being that if we took the elite of Bomber Command its squadrons would be weakened so much that morale would suffer. Results would also suffer because the general standards of the Main Force would be reduced and, what was more, the leading aircraft would be singled out and plastered by flak. Such a Force, he thought, would be subject to a five or six times greater casualty rate than the rest of the Command, possibly up to 20 per cent. There were all sorts of other arguments, notably that it would interfere with the authority of the commanders in the Main Force. Eventually, 'Bert' Harris swallowed his misgivings, the Pathfinder Force was formed, and he insisted that if it had to be, he wanted me to command it. I appreciated the trust he placed in me by giving me the job. It was rather tricky because the average age of the Group Commanders in Bomber Command was around 56 at that time, and I was only 32. To appoint one so young into such a responsible position was quite a courageous thing to do.

"The Pathfinders were prepared to put into effect the remarkable devices which were being developed by the brains of the Telecommunications Research Establishment (TRE). At Great Malvern the TRE had assembled the finest bunch

Below:
The first operational sortie of World War 2 was flown by a Bristol Blenheim IV of No 139 Squadron, Wyton on 3 September 1939. Illustrated is Bristol Blenheim IV, V6240, YH-B of No 21 Squadron which failed to return from operations on 12 July 1941.

Top right:
Though outmoded for modern aerial operations by 1940, Handley Page Hampdens provided stalwart service with Bomber and, later, Coastal Commands. Hampdens of No 408 Squadron RCAF are illustrated. The nearest is P1188, EQ-K.

Centre right:
Built in greater quantity than any other British bomber, the 'Wimpy' served in myriad roles throughout 1939-45. Vickers Wellington X3763 of No 425 Squadron RCAF failed to return from Stuttgart on 14/15 April 1943.

Bottom right:
Armstrong Whitworth Whitley, another stalwart of the Command's operational strength in 1939-42.

of scientists in the country, and the things they said were possible were quite shattering to a simple soul like myself. I was a qualified wireless operator and so had a certain amount of technical knowledge, but the things they produced, including those I knew nothing about, were most encouraging and helpful to the Pathfinders. The first thing we did was to introduce tactical planning. The Force had to do the marking so we virtually had to decide the route to the target, and also decide what other targets should be attacked to distract the enemy fighters, also what route markers would be put down (genuine and fake), and so on. Not the least important was that we had to keep down the casualties of Bomber Command. Main Force crews did between 25 and 30 bombing trips and the Pathfinders did a double tour. It was to have been 60, but we eventually cut it down to 45. Some, of course, did a lot more. One chap, the record holder, did 145 bombing operations.

"With the new Force there came a change in the procedure for laying on an operation. At the time each morning that the C-in-C and his staff were deciding what the next target or targets were to be, I was in our own HQ Ops Room with my Air Staff and Intelligence Officers. We would await their decision which came via a scrambled telephone call from Air Marshal Sir Robert Saundby, the Senior Air Staff Officer. He would give us details of the squadrons to be employed, the number of aircraft, proposed timing, and so on. We would then get our own Met Officer to give his opinion as to the likely weather, and we would lay on our plan of attack. We would decide on the principal marking method and an emergency method as a matter of course, regardless of how good the forecast might be. We would then work out the route and pass everything on to Bomber Command and the Main Force Groups by teleprinter. For three-and-a-half years our Ops Room staff planned the routeing, marking, spoof raids and fighter diversions, as well as the target approach and aiming point marking. With comparatively few exceptions this applied to all Bomber Command's major targets. The results and the lower than expected casualties speak for themselves."

Above:
AVM D. C. T. Bennett AOC No 8 (PFF) Group.
IWM

12

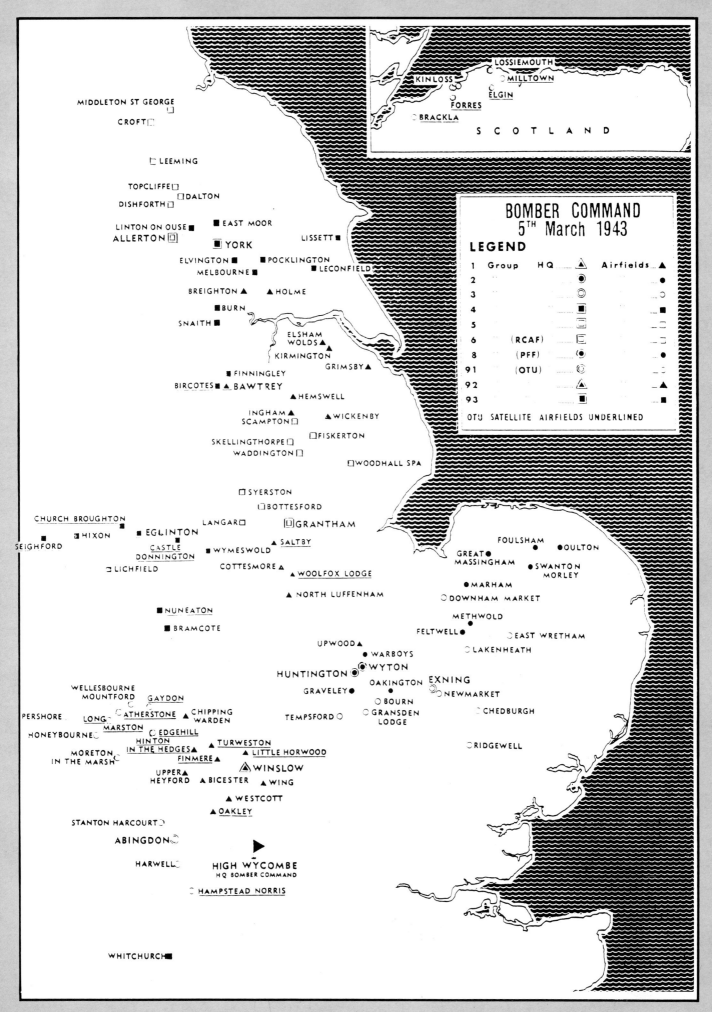

MIDDLETON ST GEORGE
CROFT

LEEMING

TOPCLIFFE
DALTON
DISHFORTH

LINTON ON OUSE ■ EAST MOOR
ALLERTON
■ YORK
LISSETT
ELVINGTON POCKLINGTON
MELBOURNE ■ LECONFIELD

BREIGHTON ▲HOLME
■BURN
SNAITH

ELSHAM
WOLDS▲
KIRMINGTON
GRIMSBY▲

FINNINGLEY
BIRCOTES ▲BAWTREY
▲HEMSWELL
INGHAM▲
SCAMPTON ▲WICKENBY

SKELLINGTHORPE FISKERTON
WADDINGTON

WOODHALL SPA

SYERSTON
BOTTESFORD

CHURCH BROUGHTON
HIXON EGLINTON LANGAR GRANTHAM
SEIGHFORD
CASTLE SALTBY
DONNINGTON WYMESWOLD
LICHFIELD COTTESMORE▲ ▲WOOLFOX LODGE

▲ NORTH LUFFENHAM

■NUNEATON
■BRAMCOTE

UPWOOD▲
● WARBOYS
HUNTINGTON WYTON
GRAVELEY● OAKINGTON EXNING
● NEWMARKET
WELLESBOURNE GAYDON BOURN
MOUNTFORD CHEDBURGH
PERSHORE ATHERSTONE ▲CHIPPING TEMPSFORD GRANSDEN
LONG WARDEN LODGE
HONEYBOURNE MARSTON
EDGEHILL RIDGEWELL
HINTON
MORETON IN THE HEDGES▲ ▲ LITTLE HORWOOD
IN THE MARSH FINMERE▲ ▲TURWESTON
UPPER▲ ▲WINSLOW
HEYFORD ▲BICESTER ▲WING
▲ WESTCOTT
▲OAKLEY
STANTON HARCOURT
ABINGDON
HARWELL ▶
HIGH WYCOMBE
HQ BOMBER COMMAND

HAMPSTEAD NORRIS

WHITCHURCH■

SCOTLAND

LOSSIEMOUTH
KINLOSS MILLTOWN
ELGIN
FORRES
BRACKLA

FOULSHAM
OULTON
GREAT SWANTON
MASSINGHAM MORLEY
MARHAM
DOWNHAM MARKET
METHWOLD
FELTWELL EAST WRETHAM
LAKENHEATH

BOMBER COMMAND
5ᵀᴴ March 1943

LEGEND

	Group		HQ		Airfields	
1	Group		▲		Airfields	▲
2			●			●
3			◎			○
4			■			■
5			⊟			⊐
6	(RCAF)		⊟			⊟
8	(PFF)		◉			●
91	(OTU)		◯			⊃
92			▲			▲
93			■			■

OTU SATELLITE AIRFIELDS UNDERLINED

BUMF-BOMBS. Loading propaganda leaflets into a Whitley. Codenamed 'Nickel', the first such 'paper-bombing' operations were flown by Whitleys of Nos 51 and 58 Squadrons on 3/4 September 1939, dropping a total of over six million leaflets (13 tons) on Hamburg, Bremen and the Ruhr complex. Note the corporal wireless operator/air gunner still wears the prewar 'brass-bullet' badge of a qualified air gunner on his tunic sleeve.

This Whitley crew of No 77 Squadron is pictured at Villeneuve, France, in early 1940 after an operational sortie. Left to right: B. D. Cayford (later DFC); LAC M. Briggs (later Flt Lt, DSO, DFC, DFM); Sgt T. G. 'Hamish' Mahaddie (later Gp Capt, DSO, DFC, AFC); AC1 Groom; Sgt 'Spike' Edmunds.

Left:
A No 9 Squadron crew prepare to don flying kit prior to an op.

Below:
Fairey Battles of No 226 Squadron, Harwell in early 1939. Already obsolete, Battles of No 1 Group were to suffer appalling casualties in France during 1939-40.

Above:
**Architect of victory: MRAF Sir Arthur Harris,
pictured at the Dorchester Hotel in 1966 to
celebrate the 20th anniversary of the
Pathfinder Association and Club.
AVM Donald Bennett is on the left, the author
on the right.** *Author*

2
'Go Get Yourself a Crew'

It has been said that the bond which existed among the members of a bomber crew was as close as a typical happy family. It certainly applied to the Thorne crew, in spite of what seemed to be a complete lack of method in the crewing-up process.

In 1943, after completing 18 months as a flying instructor on single-engined aircraft, Sgt Thorne had been posted to RAF Cranwell on a course which included navigation, aircraft basic engineering, meteorology, and flying twin-engined aircraft. After all that came conversion on to twin-engined Whitleys at RAF Forres in Scotland (a satellite of No 19 OTU, Kinloss) and Halifaxes at RAF Rufforth in Yorkshire. On arriving at Forres he was one of about 20 pilots told to find themselves a crew from a mixed bag of more than 100 navigators, wireless operators, bomb aimers and air gunners, each of whom had been told to find himself a pilot! It seemed a haphazard way to achieve a vitally important objective, a hit-or-miss gamble with long odds against six strangers coming together in the hope that they would prove compatible in all the qualities – technical and personal – necessary in the make-up of a bomber crew. In the event, the gamble came off, with the numbers of crews who quickly established an efficient and harmonious relationship far outnumbering the comparative few for whom events would prove had not been so lucky in their choice of partners.

Thorne had not rushed in to comply with the 'form-a-crew' instructions, and two days had elapsed during which he had not even approached anyone with the suggestion that they might consider risking their lives with him. By that time many crews had been formed, and he was beginning to regret the 'wait-and-see' attitude he had adopted. Then fate took a hand when two officers approached him and asked if he had completed his crew. Graham Rose, a navigator, and Boris Bressloff, a navigator/radar operator, had through no fault of their own arrived at Forres two days later than the main intake for the course. Furthermore, they had been talking to a wireless operator, Jim Crabtree, and an air gunner, Jim Raymont, neither of whom had so far committed themselves. There was immediate rapport between Thorne,

Rose and Bressloff, and if it could be extended to include the other two there remained only one more air gunner to complete the crew.

A call to the Sergeants' Mess brought out Crabtree and Raymont; within half-an-hour they were all on Christian name terms, and before the day was out Raymont had found a second air gunner in Jock Scott, a young Glaswegian who had been recommended to him by the Station Gunnery Leader. Thorne could scarcely believe his luck: he had not had to *choose* anyone, but within two days the crew of six made their first flight together in a Whitley. Not one of them including Thorne, had experience in combat flying, but all were well qualified in their respective jobs, and between them they had amassed more than 3,000hr in flying time.

Graham Rose, Boris Bressloff and Jim Crabtree formed the navigation team. Rose had interrupted an academic career to qualify as a navigator at the age of 32. Unassuming, with a quiet sense of humour, he could not have had a better partner than Bressloff. The alliance would not have come about, however, if Hitler had not invaded Russia in 1942. Bressloff, 10 years younger than Rose, had volunteered for aircrew in 1940, but he was not accepted because his father, who for many years had been – and still was – hairdresser at the Ritz Hotel in London, was of Russian birth. It was not until the USSR found itself as one of our Allies that Boris, himself a hairdresser in a famous Berkeley Square salon, was accepted for training as a bomb-aimer, followed by an observer's navigation and radar course. He was commissioned in 1943 and then went on a three-month RAF Regiment assault course and an advanced ship recognition course at Scapa Flow. His eventual posting to an OTU was proof that the 'powers-that-be' had not run out of their supply of courses, by which time he must have been one of the most versatile members of aircrew in Bomber Command.

Jim Crabtree, the third link in the navigation team, had been a policeman in Bournemouth, and he had obtained leave of absence to join the RAF as a wireless operator. Crabtree, Rose and Bressloff worked together as an ideal navigation team in training, and subsequently on the

squadron, until their 17th operation when disaster struck in a manner which will be explained later.

Apart from their highly efficient prowess as air gunners, there could not have been two more contrasting personalities than those presented by Jim Raymont and Jock Scott. The former was the 'daddy' of them all. Born in 1905, he must have been one of the oldest among the gunners in Bomber Command, and was very precise in everything that he did – a quality probably emanating from his peacetime occupation as a skilled jewellery technician and watch-maker in Birmingham. A keep-fit enthusiast, he was also a member of the Midlands Gymnastic Squad in the 1928 Olympic Games. By contrast, his opposite number, Jock Scott, was barely out of his teens. A typical 'cap-on-the-side-of-his-head' Scot, he was always ready for an argument on any subject, except during the hours in the mid-upper turret when his use of the intercom was always confined to terse but informative comments on the prevailing action. The Whitleys, of course, did not have mid-upper turrets so on all the flights from Forres the two gunners took turns in the rear turret 'to get the feel of things', as one of the gunnery instructors described it.

Scotland in midwinter is not the most pleasant area in the British Isles for flying, especially in the mountainous northern regions, and in Whitleys long past their prime. Most of the 100-plus hours flown by the crews on the course by day and night were undertaken in conditions of fog, extreme cold with periods of icing, and the odd snowstorm. Thanks to the unceasing and expert work of the groundcrews, however, there were few problems with the serviceability of the aircraft, and the aircrews themselves became quite attached to their Whitleys. But they still looked forward to the day when they would be qualified to fly in a less ponderous and more comfortable aircraft with the luxury of two engines on either side of them. That day seemed a long time in coming. Because of the weather which did not start to show any improvement until winter had been replaced by a rather tentative spring, it was not until late in March that the crews who had proved themselves capable of handling the twin-engined Whitleys were pro-

nounced ready to go on to four-engined aircraft.

There had been much to assimilate during their course at No 19 OTU apart from the actual flying. Pilots, navigators, wireless operators and air gunners had spent many hours at lectures concerning their responsibilities as far as the standards required in their respective 'trades' were concerned, and even more time was given to their working successfully as operational crews. Then, at last, the day came when they were given a date for posting to their next and, for most of them, the final conversion unit, for a course on four-engined aircraft.

The Thorne crew was one of six crews posted to No 1663 Heavy Conversion Unit at Rufforth, a RAF station seven miles west of York. Everyone went on seven days' leave, their first in four months, at the end of which they travelled separately to York where Thorne was commissioned as Pilot Officer. On a day towards the end of May 1944, they made their first flight in a Halifax. Here was luxury indeed. Massive outside, and spacious within, it was almost awe-inspiring compared with the old Whitleys, added to which there was the surging power of its four Rolls-Royce Merlin engines. After four days of lectures covering the art, for want of a better word, of flying a four-engined aircraft and the operational procedures relevant to each member of the crew, they made their first

take-off under the instruction of Flg Off Thackeray who had been screened (rested from ops) after completing a tour of 25 operations with a Halifax squadron in Yorkshire. To Thorne's surprise and relief, the transition from twins to four engines was not so complicated as he had expected, and a similar opinion was voiced by the rest of the crew so far as their work was concerned.

It was at Rufforth that they met a visiting officer who was always – and still is – described as one of the most colourful characters in Bomber Command. Wg Cdr T. G. 'Hamish' Mahaddie DSO, DFC, AFC, had joined the RAF as a Halton apprentice before the war, eventually to become No 1 Personnel Officer at Pathfinder HQ after a long and distinguished career. The purpose of his visit to Rufforth was to give a talk to the crews on the course of Pathfinder organisation and techniques. It was typical of his style that he commenced by telling his audience of a raid in which the Pathfinders went wrong. When he confessed that he was one of the people concerned in the fiasco, everyone warmed to him immediately. Some of them were so impressed by his presentation that they received with enthusiasm his subtly interpolated hints that PFF would consider applications from suitable types who might wish to join the Force. But he emphasised that only volunteers who were prepared to embark on a minimum of 45 operations would be accepted for a special Pathfinder course at the PFF Navigation Unit at RAF Warboys in Huntingdon.

Before dinner that evening Thorne, Rose and Bressloff met Hamish in the Mess and it was only natural that the conversation would get around to the subject of his afternoon talk. Thorne asked him what his idea of 'suitable types' might be. He replied: 'First, as I said in my talk, they must be volunteers with a fair amount of flying experience'. Then, looking at Thorne and Rose he said: 'Very often they are older types'. They had often discussed the possibility of volunteering for PFF and it seemed almost preordained that the opportunity should have occurred for them to meet and talk with Hamish. As the evening wore on they had been joined by others in the Mess and a real party had developed with a fund of anecdotes coming from Hamish about the funny things that had happened on his way from Halton apprentice to his wartime rank.

Two weeks later, after returning from end of course leave, the Thorne crew were on their way to RAF Warboys and on arrival they were taken for an interview with the Station Commander. Upon entering his office they were met with the greeting: 'Well, we meet again'. Gp Capt Hamish Mahaddie, had been appointed to his new command a few days earlier.

Before the crew had gone on leave, Thorne and five other pilots from Rufforth were posted for three days to go on two 'second pilot' trips with No 446 Squadron RAAF, based at Leconfield in Yorkshire. However, they all found that 'second pilot' was more of a courtesy title than anything else. Each one of them spent the whole of both trips sitting on a temporary seat next to the pilot, the idea being that the pilots should gain some inkling of what to expect on an actual operation so that they could impart something of what they had learned to their crews when they rejoined them. The Halifax crew in which Thorne found himself a passive member were all Australians. He was immediately impressed with the air of quiet confidence and efficiency — no doubt generated by their 22 previous sorties — which prevailed from the time they entered the briefing room until they returned and landed after the two operations, both of them at night.

The first on 11/12 May was a comparatively short and uneventful trip for an attack on enemy gun positions at Colline Beaumont, on the French coast. The second, on 12/13 May, was a longer and very hectic attack on the railway junction at Hasselt as part of the Allied plans to dislocate enemy communications links prior to Operation 'Overlord'. One thing that particularly impressed Thorne that night was the expert work of the two air gunners with their calm flow of information and guidance to the pilot in what seemed to be a cauldron of fire and bursting shells in the target area, and during the considerable fighter opposition on the routes from the coast and return. Two of the Australian crews went down with their aircraft that night; there was a second pilot from the Rufforth contingent in each of them.

No time was wasted at Warboys, and the organisation was such that within a period of three weeks, embryo Pathfinder crews were expected to assimilate the special techniques applicable to their job. That included reaching a standard of navigation which aimed at a tolerance of only one minute either side of the time programmed for the release of markers and bombs. On targets that could be more than four hours' flying time away, during which time there would be inevitable changes in wind force and direction, plus the hazards of searchlights, guns, enemy fighters and the changing weather conditions, a high degree of expertise and concentration was demanded of the navigators. Also, of course, the pilots had to prove they could fly a Lancaster!

On the evening after the crews' arrival at Warboys, Thorne was having a pre-dinner drink in the Mess when a wing commander came to him at the bar and without

On the evening after their arrival at RAF Warboys, Thorne was having a drink in the Mess when a wing commander came to see him and without preamble said 'You're going up with me tomorrow!' He was Wg Cdr Rodley DSO, DFC, AFC, one of the survivors of the Augsburg raid in 1942.
Wg Cdr E. E. Rodley DSO, DFC, AFC

preamble said: 'You're going up with me tomorrow'. He was Wg Cdr Rodley DSO, DFC, AFC, one of the survivors of the daylight raid by 12 Lancasters on Augsberg in 1942. (His initials are E.E. but he always says he has forgotten what they stand for, and his first name is 'Rod'.) After the war he joined Don Bennett's British South American Airways Corporation as Chief Pilot and then became Captain of BOAC's Canberra fleet.

When Rod joined the crew next morning they were driven to a dispersal where, for

the first time, they climbed the ladder into a Lancaster's fuselage. Rod settled himself into the pilot's seat with Thorne next to him on a temporary fold-down seat. When the others in the crew had settled into their positions, and before the engines were started, he ran through some of the aircraft's various controls and their locations: trimming tabs, undercarriage control, flaps, bomb doors, throttles, mixture, propellers, superchargers, radiator shutters, carburettor air intake. And he ended with the encouraging phrase so often quoted by flying instructors: 'It's a piece of cake if you know the taps'. There were many other controls concerning the fuel, oil, coolant, hydraulic, pneumatic, electrical and other systems which would be the main concern of the flight engineer, but he would be another member of the crew still to be appointed at this early stage in the pilot's conversion on to the Lancaster.

Still in the aircraft, Rod passed to the starting-up procedure: 'Test fuel pumps by the ammeter on the engineer's panel, turn ground/flight switch to "GROUND"; ground starter battery to be plugged in; confirm master engine cocks "OFF", throttles open half an inch; propeller controls fully up; slow running cut-out switches at "IDLE" position; supercharger control at "M" ratio (warning light not showing, air intake heat control at "SLOW" position); radiator shutters (override switches at "AUTOMATIC").' All those engines and checks would be the responsibility of the engineer and confirmed by verbal contact with the pilot. The engineer would also operate the fuel tank selector cocks and booster pumps, but before doing so he would be mindful of the gentle but pessimistic warning in the official *Pilot's and Flight Engineer's Notes*: 'Have a fire extinguisher ready in case of emergency'.

Nothing dramatic happened to warrant its use so at Rod's request Thorne acted as flight engineer and turned on the selector cock and master engine cock to No 2 tank, followed by the booster pump for that tank. the ignition and booster coils were then switched on and all was ready for start-up. The port inner engine was always the first to be started because it was fitted with the aircraft's generator. A trolley accumulator on the ground was used to start the engine; in fact there was a battery of accumulators in the trolley which had been plugged into the engine by the ground-crew. As soon as the engine had been started the current was generated and the charge went straight into the aircraft's batteries. Rod put his head through the open sliding window on the port side and yelled 'Contact!' to the groundcrew handling the trolley. There was an answering shout of 'Contact!' and he pressed the port engine starter button. Slowly gathering revs, with the ground-crew working away at the priming pump, the engine suddenly burst into a smooth roar which Rod reduced to a steady smooth tick-over. The other three engines were then started, the

Left and opposite:
**THE OFFICE. Pilot's instrumentation in a
Lancaster.**
IWM CH10708; drawings by Mike Keep

Below left:
**A. 'Throttles half-an-inch open; propeller
controls fully up.'** Jonathan Falconer

Below right:
B. 'Supercharger control at ''M'' ratio . . .'
Jonathan Falconer

Overleaf:
Top left:
**'. . . ignition and booster coils ON. Ready for
start-up.'** Jonathan Falconer

Bottom left:
'Contact!' Jonathan Falconer

Top right:
'Altimeter set . . .' Jonathan Falconer

Bottom right:
'. . . flaps 20 degrees down.'
Jonathan Falconer

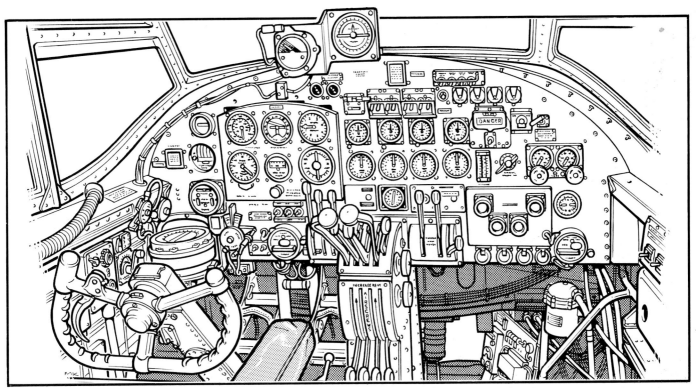

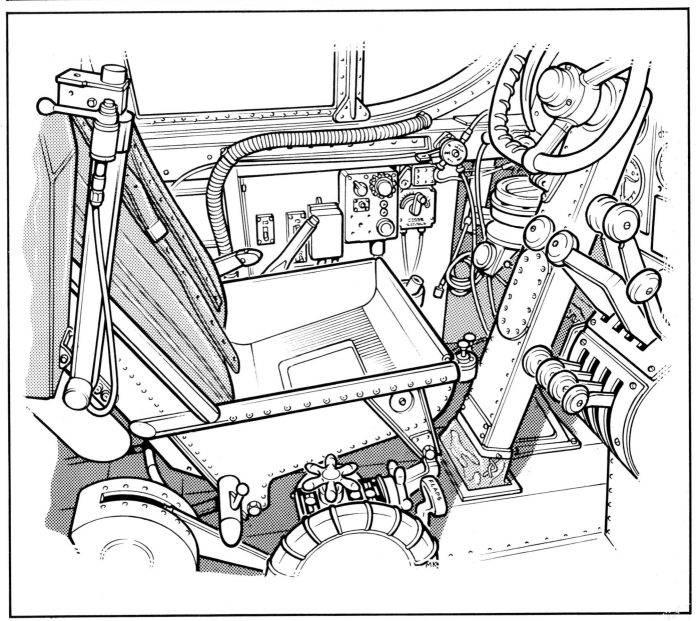

24

booster-coil switch was switched off, the ground/flight switch turned to 'FLIGHT', and ground battery removed. Each engine was then opened up slowly to 1,200rpm for warming up. Even at those low revs a minor hurricane was created to the rear, bending small trees and bushes and creating a cloud of dust.

Within five minutes they were ready to taxi to the runway for take-off; ready, that is, after the ground/flight switch was changed to 'FLIGHT', the altimeter set, the radiator shutter switches at 'OPEN' and chocks away. The aircraft was brought to a stop at the eastern end of the east/west runway. Rod called flying control and was told to take-off when ready. He checked the DR compass at 'NORMAL', the pitot head heater switch 'ON', elevator slightly forward, aileron 'NEUTRAL', propeller controls fully up, air intake at 'COLD', radiator and shutter switches at 'AUTO-MATIC', and flaps 20° down. Then turning right on to the runway, he opened the throttles to zero boost against the brakes to ensure the engines were responding evenly, throttled back, released the brakes, and then advanced the throttles. A tendency to swing to port was checked by advancing the port throttles slightly. Most pilots held their brakes on for a few seconds as they advanced the throttles at the start of take-off to provide extra power in the initial surge forward; that did help to shorten the take-off distance when the aircraft was heavily loaded, but it also increased its tendency to swing to port. It was a matter of choice, but with a light load many pilots would not use the brakes.

The Lanc's tail was soon off the ground, and with the throttles fully advanced the aircraft became airborne and the under-

carriage control was moved to the 'UP' position. Flaps were raised at 400ft and the climb continued to 2,000ft at 105mph. The electric fuel booster pumps for Nos 1 and 2 tanks had been switched off at 1,000ft at which point Rod had made a 45° turn to port. They were then heading south in the direction of the Bedford area when another 45° turn to port put them on a course towards The Wash.

Rod had not tried to blind Thorne with science, and indeed he had made the piloting of a Lanc appear a veritable 'piece of cake'. His every movement and those of the aircraft in his hands were smooth and easy, his action commentaries short and lucid. He demonstrated the effects of changes in trim with undercarriage up and down, and the effects on the nose of the aircraft (up or down) when the flaps were moved up or down in varying degrees. Approaching The Wash, he increased height to 3,000ft to demonstrate the effects from stalling. With undercarriage and flaps up, the aircraft started to stall at 110mph, and with both down the stall came at just over 90mph. In both cases there was a slight 'buffeting' but there was no tendency in either for a wing to drop. It was all very reassuring and Thorne could hardly wait to get his bottom on to the pilot's seat.

It was not a long wait. As they turned south from The Wash and headed back towards Warboys, Rod said: 'In an emergency the Lanc will maintain height at full load on any three engines at a maximum 10,000ft, and it can be trimmed to fly without using extra foot pressure from either rudder at a minimum speed of 145mph. Landing is OK with flaps at 20°. Don't lower them further until the final approach. On two engines leave the undercarriage and flaps as late as possible and glide in at around 130-135mph. If the

Below:
. . . at 1,000ft Rod made a 45 degree turn to port. *Jonathan Falconer*

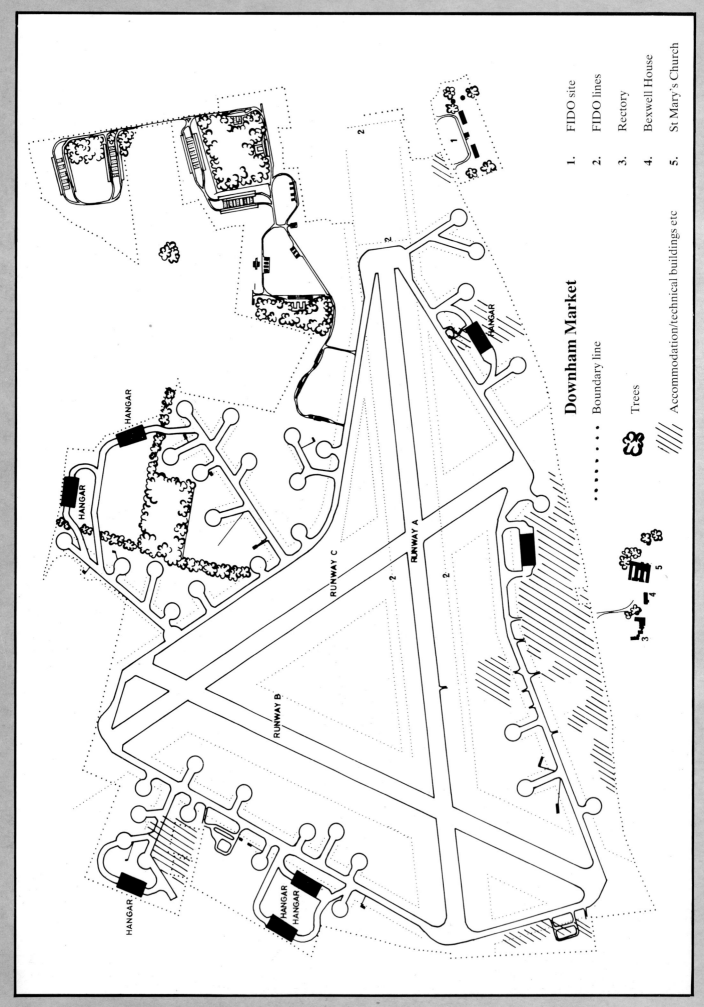

Downham Market

· · · · · · Boundary line

🌳 Trees

//// Accommodation/technical buildings etc

1. FIDO site
2. FIDO lines
3. Rectory
4. Bexwell House
5. St Mary's Church

RUNWAY A

RUNWAY B

RUNWAY C

HANGAR

two good engines are on the same side keep all turns towards them, of course'. Thorne didn't ask him what would happen if only one engine was working, but it wouldn't be very long before he was to find out.

They joined the Warboys circuit at a height of 1,000ft. Rod called flying control for permission to land and received an immediate OK. He then carried out the usual landing procedure: downwind leg reducing to 500ft, cross-wind and turn towards the runway, call position to flying control, speed 110mph, reduce engine revs and bring back control column to touchdown. And that was that! At least it was until Rod turned off the end of the runway and said : 'Right, now change seats and you have a go. Take-off and landing.' They trundled around the perimeter to the other end of the runway, took-off and repeated the 'circuit and bump' performance in complete silence until, at the point nearing the final turn on to the runway, Rod quietly suggested to Thorne that the call might be made for permission to land. That done, although rather late in the proceedings, the landing was uneventful and they taxied to the dispersal. 'Well, what do you think of her?' asked Rod. 'Lovely', replied Thorne, an opinion he was to find universal among Lancaster crews in Bomber Command.

The next afternoon the circuit performance was repeated, at the end of which Rod detached his harness from the parachute pack which formed the pilot's seat; 'There you are, it's all yours. You can break your own bloody neck but you're not going to break mine'. Then he stood up, smiled, patted Thorne on the shoulder, made his way back through the fuselage, and out.

There was hardly a spare moment for the crew during the next two weeks. When they were not flying during the day or night on mock operations — the main purpose of which was to put into practice the PFF navigation techniques which the navigation team was absorbing during lectures — Gray and Boris were not the only navigators on the course who took their work home to bed with them. 'Home' was their comfortable billet a few minutes' walk away through the woods from the Mess. Everyone had enjoyed the general atmosphere of enthusiasm and efficiency at RAF Warboys but looked forward to their final posting to an operational PFF squadron. Come to think of it, the crew seemed to have spent their time during the last seven weeks looking forward to the next move in that direction. The Lancaster itself, of course, was an important factor in their enthusiasm. The gunners welcomed their return to Fraser-Nash turrets in spite of their being slightly more cramped than in the Boulton & Paul turrets in the Halifaxes. Jim Crabtree was happy with the layout in his W/Op's compartment, and Gray and Boris didn't have time to complain about anything, so engrossed were they in being up to the minute, in more ways than one, in their navigation. And when the members of the crew who had to make their way to their places in the front of the aircraft had become accustomed to bashing their legs against the main spar — it traversed the fuselage near the W/Op's compartment — everyone agreed that the Lancaster was all that it had been cracked up to be. Then there was the seventh member of the crew.

After Wg Cdr Rodley had told Thorne what he could do with his neck, or words to that effect (they've both often laughed about it since) the crew returned to the aircraft dispersal at the end of the afternoon's unsupervised flying. A young flight sergeant who had been talking with the groundcrew came to Thorne and said: 'The engineer officer told me to come over and introduce myself to you. You'll be wanting a flight engineer, won't you?' The following night he flew with the crew on a mock operation, a three-hour flight with many changes of course taking them over Wales, north over the Pennines to 'attack' a point near Scarborough, south over The Wash and back to Warboys. By the time the first turning point had been reached it was obvious that Harry Parker knew his job and was a perfect fit so far as everyone in the crew was concerned. He had joined the RAFVR three months before his 18th birthday to train as flight mechanic and fitter, eventually to become a flight engineer. After the war he flew for two years as engineer with Gp Capt Leonard Cheshire VC in the latter's Mosquito at the time when he was setting up his Cheshire Homes in the UK and on the Continent.

At the end of the crew's second week at Warboys, the station adjutant told Thorne to warn the crew to expect a posting to a PFF squadron within four days. He did not know which one it would be but he would let him know as soon as the details came through.

There were two types of operational stations to which aircrew and ground personnel could be posted after they had passed through the various training units. It was largely a matter of luck whether they would be directed to one of the prewar stations which were reputed to contain every modern convenience within their permanent brick-built edifices; or they might find themselves deposited in a recently erected conglomeration of concrete units and Nissen huts.

RAF Downham Market came within that latter category. Information they had gleaned during the months of training had convinced them that the possibilities of a more relaxed and informal lifestyle on a newly built wartime station would be preferable to the perhaps more traditional routine of a permanent station. They let their preference be known by a spot of discreet lobbying in the right quarters,

Left:
READY TO GO. Sgt C. H. Doswell and Plt Off Jim Cowan in their No 9 Squadron Lancaster at Waddington, December 1942. *L. Brown*

Left: *High Street, Downham Market*
With the ending of the war in Europe the inhabitants of Downham Market quickly resumed their normal peacetime lives. The roar of Lancasters taking off by day and night from the airfield, little more than a mile ahead on the road in this picture of the High Street, was soon replaced by the more gentle sounds familiar to a country town.

The Crown Hotel lies behind the clock tower, with Sly's Cafe, now renamed Norfolk Kitchen, a few yards up on the left. The Castle Hotel is at the top in this picture which was taken in 1946.

Far left, below: *Bexwell Church*
Dating back to the 12th century, Bexwell Church was a haven at all times to the men and women on the squadrons, many of whom confessed that they never even thought of 'going to church' in normal times.

Below left: *The Crown Hotel*
Saturday nights were always particularly busy in the Crown when visiting dance bands, often from nearby USAAF bases, played for dances in the Town Hall, from which the Crown was just across the road.

Above right: *The Hare Arms*
Near the perimeter of the airfield, the Hare Arms lies on the road to King's Lynn. The owner was Peter Winlove-Smith, but while he was away during the war serving with Coastal Command on air-sea rescue duties fishing aircrew out of the North Sea, the 'Hare' was run by his very attractive wife who was known to all as 'Bill'. Now retired, they still live in the area.

Centre right
Another view of Downham Market High Street looking towards the Castle Hotel.

All photographs on this spread courtesy of H. Soehnle

Below: *The Castle Hotel*
Members of aircrews could sometimes arrange for their wives to travel to Downham Market when they knew they would be stood down from operations for a couple of days. The Castle Hotel specialised in providing excellent accommodation on such occasions.

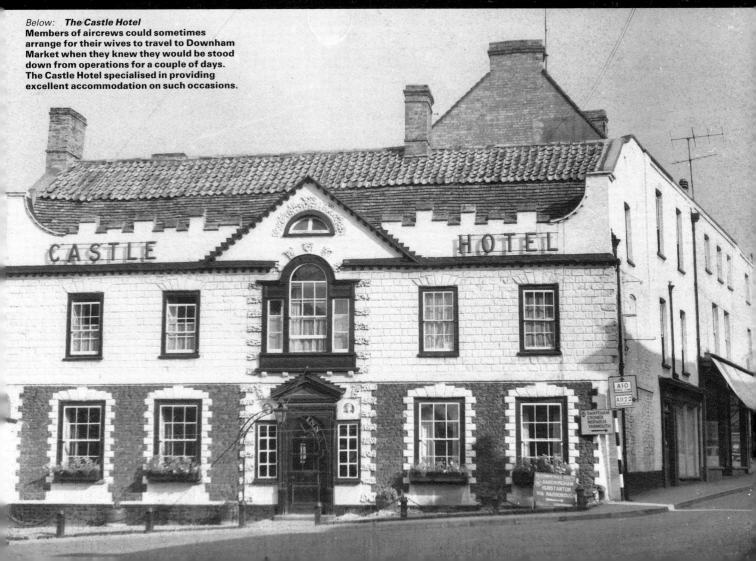

crossed their fingers and awaited the outcome. Their hopes were fulfilled and they never regretted their decision.

Situated in north Norfolk, 15 miles south of King's Lynn, the peaceful existence of Downham Market's 3,000 inhabitants had not been greatly disturbed by the war in spite of there being 17 Bomber Command airfields within a 30-mile radius of the town. The area differed from much of the county's terrain in that it consisted of reasonably undulating and well-wooded country. There was, however, a plateau of farmland to the north of the town and in 1942 work began on transforming that area into a bomber station. By the end of the year three runways had been laid with 36 aircraft dispersal points, and all the buildings and installations necessary for the functioning of an operational station had been completed or were nearing completion. Where cattle had grazed for centuries the scene changed to a landscape of hangars, bomb dumps and petrol storage tanks, squadron offices and other administrative buildings, messes and living quarters, control tower, radio and radar establishments – and a cinema. It was not long before the roar of aircraft taking-off and landing by day and night, to say nothing of the rumble of heavy traffic through the main street, created a new and noisy background to their lives. They were not alone among the towns and villages of Britain which accepted a similar sudden change with a warm-hearted cheerfulness, and they soon became the friends of the men and women of the squadrons who were to come.

The first squadrons to make Downham Market their homes were Nos 214 and 218, flying Short Stirlings. They were 'heavy' bombers in every sense of the word. Bigger and heavier than any of their predecessors, they looked well-nigh indestructible.

Unfortunately for those who had to fly them, the Stirling's performance did not match up to its size. No one among the aircrews who survived the eccentricities encountered in take-offs and landings, and the long struggles to reach a maximum ceiling of even 12,000ft with a bomb load, shed any tears when they were taken out of operational service.

Fortunately, the build-up of Bomber Command had been steadily increasing in 1941, including the introduction of two new four-engined aircraft – the Handley Page Halifax in March and the Avro Lancaster in December – the latter being later acclaimed as 'the finest in the war' by Air Marshal Arthur Harris who was appointed C-in-C, Bomber Command on 23 February 1942. Strangely, the Lancaster's pedigree could not have been more questionable. Since 1936 designers and manufacturers had been struggling to produce a twin-engined bomber capable of carrying a 12,000lb bomb load. This was the Avro Manchester, the first example making its first test flight on 25 July 1939, by which date production was already underway in the factories. The Manchester commenced its operational career in February 1941 but nothing seemed to go right, and the design's shortcomings called for continued mechanical and structural

alterations. Yet despite all that it was generally agreed that the basic design was sound – it simply needed more powerful (and reliable) engines. Crews were taking-off knowing that if they 'lost' one engine, as they often did, it would be almost impossible to remain airborne. Soon Manchesters became a grim joke among aircrews who did not have to fly them, with the word going round that the best attended social events in PoW camps were the reunions organised by shot-down Manchester aircrews!

Nevertheless, the Manchester's deficiency in engine power and reliability had been recognised by its designers as early as 1939, when several variant designs, employing two or four other types of engine, were projected, including a 'Manchester Mk III' with four Rolls-Royce Merlins. In the event, a standard Manchester airframe was modified to accept four Merlins and this first flew in January 1941, and later entered full production as the Lancaster.

In June 1942 all Manchesters were withdrawn from service as bombers after what was officially admitted to have been 'a brief and disastrous operational career'. Nevertheless, as Harris said later: 'If there had been no Manchester, Bomber Command would never have had the Lancaster'.

On 25 July the crew travelled by train to Downham Market where they were met at the station in the early evening of a perfect summer day by the WAAF driver of a RAF station runabout. She drove them through the typical Norfolk small town pointing out local landmarks such as the Town Hall, the Crown and Castle hotels, Sly's Bakery and Café, the Hare Inn and other local spots which were to provide many happy periods in their off-duty hours during the months to come.

The drive to the airfield did not take more than 10 minutes before they came to a stop outside the main Flight offices just a few yards from the airfield's perimeter track. A flight lieutenant came out of one of the concrete single-storey buildings. 'Hello', he said 'my name's Norman Page. I'm the adjutant. Welcome to 635 Squadron. Come into my office and we'll go through the usual new arrivals bumff. Leave your gear in the wagon and it can go with you to your quarters when we are finished.'

There were not enough chairs in his office for everyone but it took only a few minutes for him to check their individual details. Then he gave a shout 'Flight', and within a few seconds the door opened and his flight sergeant entered. 'Will you take these gentlemen to their quarters, you know which they are, and then show them how to get to the Officers' and Sergeants' Messes.' Then turning to Thorne he added, 'I'll see you in the Mess bar in, say, an hour'.

They all climbed back into the runabout and were driven past the guard room and through the open gates, over the Bexwell Road and up the lane to the XIIth century church nestling among the trees. There they stopped. The officers amongst them collected their belongings and followed their flight sergeant guide past the vicarage next to the church and into the orchard behind. He then identified their quarters, one of a dozen Nissen huts in the orchard which still had some of its orginal trees bearing fruit. This was where the officers and NCOs in the crew parted company for a while, the latter to go on to their quarters which were about a quarter-of-a-mile away up the lane.

'Nissen hut' sounds pretty basic but Gray, Boris and Thorne were pleasantly surprised when they went inside. It was spacious and bright with what appeared to be comfortable beds, each with a wooden chest of drawers and a chair. As they were sorting out their baggage the door opened and in came an airman who introduced himself as 'Jimmy, the hut orderly or batman or whatever you like to call me. I expect you'd like some hot water, then I'll leave you to unpack.' As Gray said, it all looked very promising.

They met the adjutant as arranged and after dinner they sought out the other four members of the crew from the NCOs' Mess. Although darkness had fallen, it was a warm clear night so they had a wander around the 'domestic area' as it was called. In addition to the Officers', NCOs' Airmen's and WAAFs' Messes, there were the medical quarters, hospital, and the station cinema, all within an area of a quarter-of-a-mile. As they stood in the lane and looked down on the airfield which they could just discern about half-a-mile away and some 50ft below them, the perimeter lights came on. Almost immediately it became alive with cars and wagons which could clearly be seen racing to various points around the perimeter. It was not long before the familiar roar of Lancaster engines, increasing in volume, vibrated around them. The night was so clear that even in the darkness they could pick out the aircraft as they joined the circuit and were marshalled by ground control to land on the long east-west runway. The pilot in the first aircraft made his final turn towards the runway, on came the beam of the aircraft's landing light and as he touched down and settled on the runway he increased the engine revs and hurried safely toward the far end to clear for his colleagues following. They had taken-off four hours earlier to lead a raid on the manufacturing and coal-producing areas at Saarbrücken in West Germany.

Six aircraft had taken-off, and six returned. It was an impressive end to the day for the Thorne crew.

The following morning Thorne was directed to the 'C' Flight office to meet the Flight Commander, Sqn Ldr Hugh 'Pat' Connolly, a renegade Irishman as he described himself. There were three Flights in the squadron each with up to 10 or 12 crews. In many ways Pat was not unlike Hamish Mahaddie and a most popular character in the squadron. Like Hamish, he too had joined the RAF in prewar days and had earned similar rapid promotions. After the war he became an Air Commodore, commanding RAF Biggin Hill and Halton. He introduced Thorne to the crew captains who were present and to those who popped into and out of the office during the morning. They were a jovial crowd, aged in their mid-twenties to mid-thirties, but it was soon apparent that behind the prevailing air of informality there was the assurance and enthusiasm of airmen who knew what they were doing. The crew spent the afternoon and the following day familiarising themselves with the general organisation of the squadron with unaccompanied visits to the various sections – navigation, gunnery, engineering, radio, met, and flying control. Pat Connolly had said that if the squadron was operating on the following day or night they would probably be on the battle order. That was confirmed the next morning and at 22.56hrs on 28 July the crew took-off on their first operation – to Hamburg.

After the Thorne crew had returned from their seventh operation with No 635 Squadron (it was to Stettin in Poland) the squadron commander told Thorne that the crew would finish their stint as Supporters (crews which went in first over the target and draw enemy fire away from the master bomber and his deputy) as soon as he could fix them up with a bomb aimer who would complete the crew as Visual Centrers. Two weeks later WO Reg Keary joined the crew. After qualifying as an air observer in South Africa in 1942 he returned to the UK and was posted to No 419 Squadron at RAF Middleton St George. On his second operation two of the crew were killed and after 24 ops with further misfortunes, including two crash-landings, the crew were taken off operational flying. Reg was then appointed bombing instructor at RAF Lossiemouth. After a year he volunteered for PFF, ultimately to become one of the family in the Thorne crew. Later, he was commissioned, as also was Jim Raymont.

Left:
The ill-starred Avro Manchester entered squadron service with No 207 Squadron in November 1940, flew its first operations on 24/25 February 1941, and its ultimate operations on 25/26 June 1942.

Avro Lancaster prototype, BT308, which was initially issued to No 44 Squadron on 16 September 1941 for crew conversion training.

Right:
On the morning following their arrival at Downham Market, the Thorne crew were directed to No 635 Squadron's 'C' Flight office to meet the Flight Commander, Sqn Ldr Hugh 'Pat' Connolly DFC, AFC, AFM. An ex-Halton aircraft apprentice, he later rose to the rank of Air Cdre and was Commandant of Halton at the time of his death in 1968. *IWM CH16176*

Below:
BOMBER BARONS. Only volunteers prepared to embark on a minimum of 45 operations were accepted for service with the PFF. Some got the 'chop' fairly soon after joining; many went on to complete a full tour; others embarked on a second tour. Leading PFF pilots, from left to right: Gp Capt J. Searby, DSO, DFC; Wg Cdr S. P. 'Pat' Daniels DSO, DFC; Gp Capt R. W. P. Collings DSO, DFC; Gp Capt T. G. Mahaddie DSO, DFC, AFC; AVM D. C. T. Bennett CB, CBE, DSO with MRAF Lord Tedder, at a postwar function. *Gp Capt T. G. Mahaddie*

Facing page, top:
Sqn Ldr Alec Cranswick DSO, DFC completed 104 operations before his death on 4/5 July 1944 over Villeneuve St Georges in Lancaster ND846, TL-J of No 35 Squadron PFF. It was to Cranswick that AVM Don Bennett dedicated his autobiography. *IWM CH10641*

Facing page, bottom:
Sqn Ldr Danny Everett DFC (Two Bars), seen here as a sergeant with members of his first operational crew, completed 98 operational sorties, was then *ordered* to cease operational flying, but wangled one more trip with No 35 Squadron skippering a scratch crew on 7 March 1945 — and failed to return. *Mrs F. Bennett*

Bombing Techniques

In the early days of the Pathfinders the attack was led by an experienced pilot and crew who had proved their efficiency in marking a target with coloured flares to give the Main Force which was following an aiming point for their bombs. He then controlled the progress of the attack by radio. He was given the title of Master Bomber and in case anything disastrous happened to him he had a Deputy Master Bomber in another aircraft who could take over. In order to provide them with some support, and not to leave them as easy targets for the ground defences, they were accompanied by crews who were in the early stages of their tour in PFF. They carried bombs only and no marker flares, or Target Indicators (TIs) as they were called. The TIs came in a variety of colours and combinations of colours for each raid so that the enemy did not have time to throw down spoof markers to mislead the Main Force. When a crew had proved their worth, they graduated from Supporters to Visual Centrers (originally named Backers-Up). They were spaced within the Main Force so that there would be a continuity of new markers to replace those that were losing their brilliance on the ground. When necessary they adjusted their aim according to radio instructions from the Master Bomber, and the Main Force did the same.

After Oboe and H2S were introduced, a daylight attack commenced with PFF Mosquitos flying high above the heavies; they dropped their marker flares on the target area as indicated by their radar instruments, the Deputy Master Bomber then went in and released his markers, followed by the Master Bomber who

assessed the accuracy of the marking. From then on he circled the area broadcasting instructions to the Visual Centrers and the Main Force. Other marking techniques were introduced for times when it was difficult or impossible to identify the target because of weather conditions. One of them, codenamed 'Wanganui', the home town in New Zealand of Sqn Ldr 'Artie' Ashworth, an Air Staff Officer at Pathfinder HQ and later a pilot in No 635 Squadron. 'Wanganui' marking was employed when the ground was totally obscured by thick cloud through which even the glow of marker flares could not be seen. The target area would be identified by Oboe, or by H2S if it was out of the range of Oboe, then 'Blind

Markers' in PFF Lancasters would drop flares on parachutes at a height and position above the cloud calculated to provide what in effect would be aiming points in the sky on an invisible target on the ground. The idea was received with incredulous laughter in some quarters but it proved remarkably effective.

Below:
The ubiquitous de Havilland Mosquito — the 'Wooden Wonder' — made its operational debut in Bomber Command on 31 May 1942 and became a major weapon in the Command's 'armoury': exemplified here with Mosquito PF432, 'W' of No 128 Squadron at Wyton about to receive a 4,000lb HC/HE 'Cookie' bomb for a raid on Berlin on 21 March 1945.

Now Thrive the Armourers

ERKS. A typical batch of the unpublicised —
and rarely honoured — groundcrews who
'kept 'em flying'; in this case with 'their'
Lancaster after its return from bombing Berlin
on 18 January 1943.   *IWM CH8484*

Above:
WOMEN'S LIB. 1943-style. A WAAF driver delivers a train of bomb trolleys to a dispersal. Formed initially on 28 June 1939, the Women's Auxiliary Air Force (WAAF) reached its peak numerical strength of 181,835 (all ranks) on 1 July 1943; while by December 1945 an overall total of 217,249 women had served.

Right:
Armourers beavering in the bomb dump prior to a night's ops, here preparing Small Bomb Containers (SBCs) filled with 4lb incendiary bombs. *IWM CH10709*

Facing page, top:
A trolley-load of 500lb MC/HE bombs being loaded into a Lanc at Metheringham for a raid on Frankfurt, 22/23 March 1944. The number '43' chalked on bomb noses referred to the type of bomb pistol fitted in the nose of each bomb. *IWM CH12541*

Facing page, bottom:
FIRE LOAD. An armourer resting on SBCs while refuelling is completed. Each SBC contained 4lb incendiary bombs.

40

Lancaster R5868, PO-S, 'Sugar' of No 467
Squadron RAAF, Waddington on 10 May
1944, with its intended load of one 4,000lb
HC/HE 'Cookie' and assorted 500lb MC/HE
bombs. This Lancaster is now in the Bomber
Command Museum at Hendon, London, fully
restored.

Left:
Bomb bay of R5868, PO-S of No 467 Squadron RAAF, Waddington on 11 May 1944 prior to a raid on Bourg-Leopold that night. A 4,000lb HC/HE 'Cookie' blast bomb nestles among clutches of 500lb MC/HE bombs.

Below left:
An alternative bomb load for a Lancaster: 12 × 500lb Cluster canisters containing incendiary bombs.

Right:
Feeding the nose guns of Lanc ED763, of No 617 Squadron at Woodhall Spa, in 1944. Total capacity was 14,000 rounds.
IWM CH18175

Left:
COOKIE. A 4,000lb HC/HE blast bomb is 'ridden' by an engineering officer and (right) Wg Cdr W. J. R. Shepherd OBE, the No 8 Group PFF Intelligence Officer at Graveley, early in 1944. In the background is Mosquito BIV, DZ637 of No 692 Squadron. *Hawker-Siddeley*

Below:
Another view of Mosquito BIV, DZ637 of No 692 Squadron, about to be loaded with a 4,000lb HC/HE 'Cookie' bomb.

Above:
Installing 0.303in calibre Browning machine guns into a No 50 Squadron Lanc's tail turret. Note flash eliminators affixed to muzzles.

Right:
Other essential groundcrew services included replenishment of oxygen, as pictured here on Lanc ZN-D of No 106 Squadron, Metheringham in 1944. *IWM CH10033*

Below:
Bombing-up and refuelling Lanc LM130, JO-N of 'A' Flt No 463 Squadron, at Waddington (pilot Flg Off Hattam, RAAF), which displays a bomb log of 61 sorties already completed. Ultimately it crashed at Metheringham on 11 March 1945. *S. Bridgeman*

Above:
Refuelling a No 50 Squadron Lanc, while nearby SBCs or incendiaries await their turn to be loaded.

Left:
PROP CHANGE. 'L-for-Leather' of No 431 Squadron RCAF at Croft in 1945. *RCAF*

Above:
Flt Sgt Gordon Cooper, a WOp/AG with 24 operations 'under his belt', helps LACW Radford with a parachute at Fiskerton on 20 December 1943. *IWM CH12050*

Right:
Fiskerton Flying Control Room on the night of 2/3 January 1944. From left to right: Flt Lt L. Bone; ?; ?; Cpl Brown, WAAF and AC1 K. G. Clarke. *IWM CH12207*

3
The Lanc That Nearly Made It

'Happy Valley' was the name given by Bomber Command crews to the Ruhr area of the Rhine. It was typical of their ironic sense of humour because from the spring of 1940 it was anything but a happy place for them. From Dortmund down to Cologne there were massive conglomerations of factories producing a major part of the enemy's supplies of war materials, from guns to submarines, tanks, aircraft, oil; and munitions from bullets to bombs. Dortmund, Duisberg, Düsseldorf, and Cologne were among the names announced with monotonous regularity as the target for the night. But for most of the crews the name they least wanted to hear at a briefing was Essen, for nearly a century the home of the giant Krupps armaments empire.

For more than two years from the start of the war, 10% of Bomber Command attacks had been on Essen and it would not be an overstatement to say that it was the target most feared by the crews. The story

went around that one brave member of Headquarters staff made the comment to 'Bomber' Harris that the aircrews were getting fed up with going to Essen night after night. 'So is Essen', was the curt reply. As AVM Don Bennett has explained, the losses among aircrew continued to be heavy and without any significant effect on enemy production. Heavy and light gun batteries were massed in and around the city and its factories, and with only the basic navigation aids available at the time the crews found it impossible to identify individual targets through the industrial haze and smoke which always lay over the Ruhr valley. But still they pressed on without much reward until the advent of new navigation aids and a 'new look' in Bomber Command's strategy and tactics which were introduced during the latter part of 1942.

The Thorne crew had completed 15 operations with No 635 Squadron with a daylight attack on the submarine pens at

Bergen on the west coast of Norway, on 4 October 1944. Seven of those ops had been to targets in the Ruhr, including two on Essen, and two on Gelsenkirchen. The latter were undertaken in daylight, and for Thorne's money — and the crew's — they were the most dicey of all, including Essen. Gelsenkirchen was an industrial town with oil production plants, collieries and iron works. Each of the routes to Gelsenkirchen had taken them over Tilburg in the south of Holland. From there to the target, a distance of just over 100 miles, there had been considerable opposition from enemy fighters, and from the ground defences in

Below:
Of the Thorne crew's first 15 ops with No 635 Squadron, seven had been to targets in the Ruhr including two on Essen, which had been the most dicey of all. In this night attack on Essen, 11 March 1945, 'Window' anti-radar foil is dropped to confuse German defences.
IWM CH5635

the form of heavy and light flak. The fighters, especially in daylight, were always a menace and the effectiveness of a bomber's defence against them depended entirely upon the tactics employed by the bomber's crew.

Frank Kelsh, No 635 Squadron gunnery leader, had always impressed upon his gunners that they were not there to engage in a shooting match with the Luftwaffe. Their job was to help get the aircraft to the target and home again with the least possible trouble. They should avoid direct combat by giving their pilots the earliest possible warning of a fighter which could be taking a special interest in their aircraft. If an attack did develop following a danger warning over the intercom from one of the gunners, it was up to the pilot to 'lose' the fighter by correctly-timed evasive action which usually took the form of a tight corkscrew in the direction from which the fighter was coming in. If that could be accomplished successfully on two separate attacking runs by the fighter pilot, it was possible he would break off and seek an easier prey. To assist the gunners in maintaining a look-out for enemy fighters, it was an accepted tactic for the pilot to manoeuvre his aircraft into a continuous gentle weave, at the same time as an equally gentle up-and-down switchback movement. That gave the gunners an opportunity to see below the aircraft, the favourite position for a fighter commencing an attack, and the most dangerous for the

bomber. If a fighter could spot a bomber just stooging along serenely on a steady course, he would creep up from below and astern. The first warning that the gunners would get was likely to be the fuselage being filled with bursting cannon shells and machine-gun bullets.

A certain amount of luck was vital for survival in any form of combat in war, but luck had to be with you 100% if you were to get through the flak from the guns of the ground defences. There were some pilots who had come safely through a succession of operations wondering if they had developed a form of extra-sensory perception in avoiding parts of the sky where sudden explosions of black smoke would appear from the bursting shells. But the explosions were unpredictable and their victims were as likely to be old hands nearing the end of their tour, or a crew on their first op.

D-Dog had landed from the Bergen trip at 12.20hrs. The flight had taken exactly eight hours from start to finish in glorious weather and in truth it had been enjoyable, if that word is appropriate applied to such a mission. After debriefing and lunch the crew were ready for their first spot of sleep in 19hr. They had been told that they would be stood down next day but that they might be on a battle order for the next night. After finishing their lunch they felt refreshed, and so they decided to take a shower, dress and go to Sly's Café for tea, then early to bed so as to be fit for the next

night if they were on the battle order. In any case they would go in the morning to their respective Flight offices and follow with a visit to D-Dog, see the groundcrew and carry out an aircraft check in readiness for either a night op or perhaps another in daylight on the following day, 6 October. According to plan they were all up, and at 9am in the offices of the leaders of their respective 'trades' — navigation, engineering, bombing and gunnery. This was the normal procedure for all aircrew personnel and not just those who were on the day's or night's battle orders. Pilots met in their own Flight office to hear and to discuss the latest gen from Pathfinder headquarters and from their own squadron CO.

Below:
OPPONENT 1: Focke Wulfe Fw190A-4 of 11/JG2.

Right:
OPPONENT 2: Junkers Ju88G-7A of the crack nightfighter unit I/NJG 100.

Below right:
OPPONENT 3: Messerschmitt Bf110G-4 from NJG6 which landed in Switzerland on 15 March 1944. The nose housed a fairly typical FuG202 radar display.

Pre-flight checks

When Thorne arrived at D-Dog's dispersal, Jim Raymont was already there and halfway through checking the four Mk 2 Browning guns in his rear turret. They had been cleaned and checked earlier by the armourers in the groundcrew and Jim's main pre-flight operation was to harmonise the four guns so that their fire was concentrated on one aiming point and not individually firing all over the sky. To do that he had to first climb from the inside of the fuselage into his turret — and that was easier said than done — then he sat down and centralised the turret. By removing the breech blocks from the guns he was able to look down each barrel towards a board half as big again as a school blackboard which one of the groundcrew had mounted on an easel 40ft to the rear of the aircraft. In the top left-hand corner of the board there was painted a large 'X', and an 'O' of equal size on each of the other three corners. The top left gun was fixed on its mounting and the barrel of that gun was then lined up on the 'X'. The other three guns were not fixed and could be individually adjusted to line up with the appropriate 'O' corners. They were then in their adjusted positions on their mountings. By this method the cone of fire from the four guns would converge at 400yd to the rear of the aircraft. The guns were always fed with a mixture of various types of ammunition depending upon the circumstances (whether an operation was to be by day or night for instance), and the fighter opposition expected. Four tanks were situated in the fuselage behind the gun turret and each contained 2,000 rounds of ammunition which were conveyed along metal tracks by a mechanical-hydraulic system direct to the guns as they were fired. If a gun or one of the tracks became jammed, an automatic throw-out was activated thus preventing the rounds from piling up in the turret or fuselage and allowing the other guns to continue firing. The used rounds spilled down chutes and out into the slipstream. The front gunner who was also the bomb aimer did not enjoy that facility however, and when he did fire his guns he invariably finished with spent rounds piled up around his ankles.

Above right:
'Arse-End Charlie' — a Lancaster tail gunner seated in his 'Mighty Wurlitzer'. Frank Kelsh, No 635 Squadron gunnery leader, had always impressed upon his gunners that they were not there to engage in a shooting match with the Luftwaffe, but to get their aircraft to the target and home again with the least possible trouble.

Right:
Jock Scott, mid-upper air gunner, climbed into his perspex dome where there was the luxury of a detachable swing seat. The close confines of a Lancaster's fuselage interior is demonstrated here by Plt Off J. Johnston RCAF, a mid-upper air gunner on No 619 Squadron, 14 February 1944. *IWM CH12280*

Above:
W/Op. Lancaster Wireless Operator in his 'cabin' — the warmest crew position. Squeezed into his seat, Jim Crabtree faced forward, his transmitter/receiver, Morse key, logs and charts on a small desk in front of him. *IWM CH8790*

As Thorne left Jim to get on with his harmonising and started to make his way forward up the fuselage towards the cockpit, a shout of 'Who's going flying then?' came from the outside. It was Harry Parker, who had arrived to do his flight engineer checks. Jock Scott was with him to carry out a performance on his mid-upper guns similar to that which Jim had already started in his rear turret. Jock left the other three almost immediately to climb into his perspex dome where there was the luxury of a detachable swing seat. The instruments and controls were similar to those in the rear turret but with three main differences. First, the guns traversed 360°, apart from an automatic cut-out to prevent the gunner hitting the fins and rudders at the rear of his own aircraft; second, the downward angle of fire was obviously more limited; third, there was more room and comfort than in the rear turret — but not much more.

The route to the front of the aircraft from that point was strewn with obstacles that had to be squeezed past or climbed over. On the starboard side there were ammunition chutes and storage boxes for parachutes and oxygen, and quick release fixtures for flame floats and sea markers; opposite on the port side were a reservoir and hand pump for hydraulic fluid. Also taking up a fair amount of room was what was euphemistically described as a rest bed. It was intended, of course, for use by anyone who had been injured and not for the odd crew member who might be feeling tired. Forward from there on the port side was the wireless op's 'snuggery' — a description credited to a half-frozen Lancaster gunner in the past who for some reason unknown after the passage of time had left his turret and wandered into the W/Op's compartment. The sudden change from the lonely and sub-zero conditions in his turret into an atmosphere of warmth and comparative comfort, brought tears to his eyes. Or so the story goes. In fact the interior heating in a Lancaster was a somewhat delicate matter because the heat came from the engines and entered the fuselage via the W/Op's cabin, from whence it dispersed with diminishing effect throughout the interior of the fuselage.

That meant that the rear gunner isolated in his turret did not benefit from it at all, and the mid-upper gunner fared only slightly better; the cockpit would be comfortably warm, whilst the W/Op could be nearly on the boil. As it was his responsibility to operate the heat controls he was always, one might say, in an invidious position. The space he occupied was in accord with the dictionary definition of a 'snuggery': 'sheltered from cold and wet, packed in, good enough for modest requirements'. Squeezed into his seat Jim Crabtree faced forward, his transmitter/receiver, Morse key, logs and charts were on a small desk in front of him. On the starboard side was a panel containing fuses for the electrical systems and on the fuselage on either side of him were the heat controls.

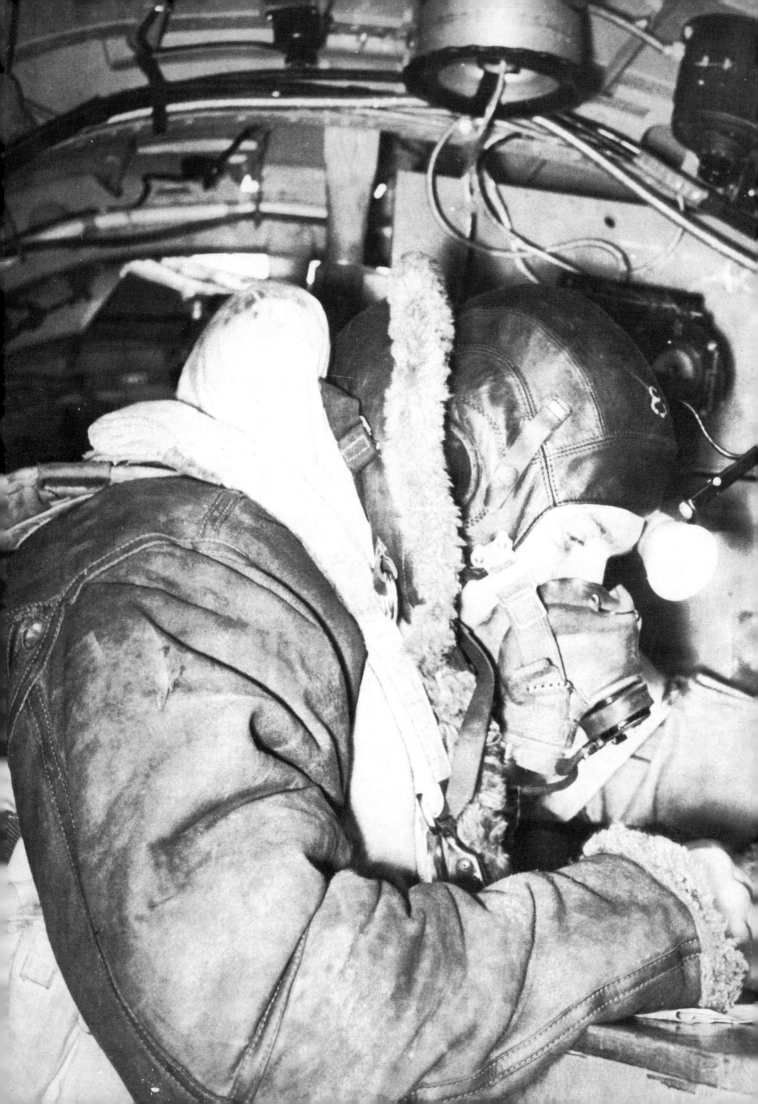

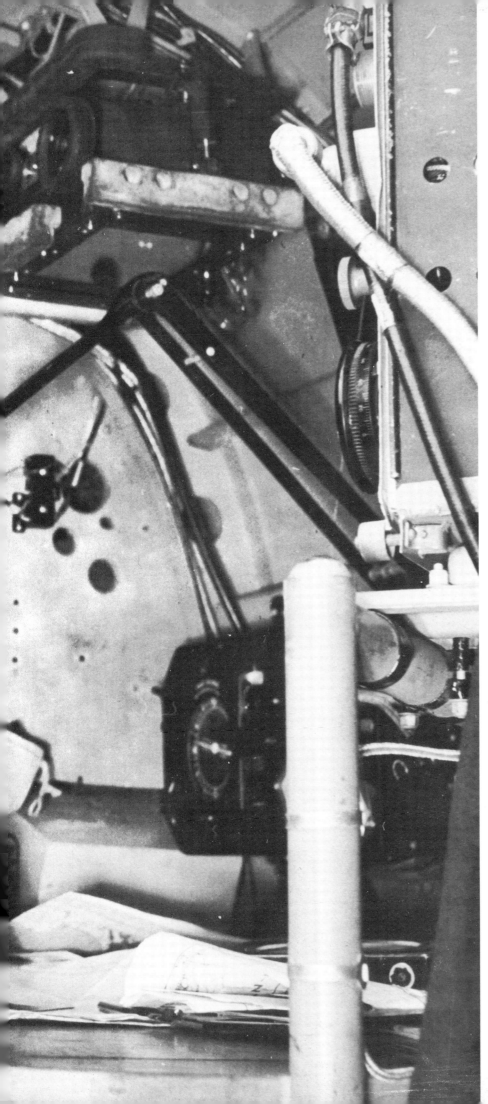

Radar aids

Immediately ahead was the cabin where Graham Rose and Boris Bressloff carried out what the latter modestly described as their navigational miracles, all of which were performed behind heavy curtains so the light they used would not shine into the cockpit and upset the pilot's night vision, as well as being a give-away to prowling enemy fighters. The navigators sat facing the inside of the port fuselage at the table containing the charts, books and instruments of their trade. Some of the pilot's instruments were duplicated here including the air speed indicator and compass. A master compass was in the rear of the fuselage. Two of their most important instruments were 'Gee' and 'H2S'. The former was an excellent aid to pinpointing the geographical position of the aircraft as indicated by signals from three widely separated transmitters based in the UK. When the difference in the times taken by the signals to reach the aircraft was revealed on the 'Gee' box and plotted by the navigator on a special chart, the aircraft's exact position could be determined. Everything depended on the expertise of the aircraft's radar set operator, and Boris was never lacking in the necessary skills. The one drawback of 'Gee' was its limited range. Reception of the transmissions started to fade from around 5° East and as the aircraft flew deeper over enemy territory the 'Gee' box became unusable.

As so often happened, the boffins at Telecommunications Research Establishment (TRE) came up with an answer. In January 1942 they produced the prototype of a new radar aid that could be operated by the set operator in an aircraft entirely independent of external power or devices. Simply, 'H2S' as it was codenamed, transmitted radio waves downwards from the aircraft. They were reflected back from the ground to show features from below (eg buildings, ships and water expanses) on the face of a cathode-ray tube in the navigators' compartment, not unlike a large photographic negative. This could be achieved by day or night irrespective of weather conditions, giving a competent operator the opportunity to pinpoint the aircraft's position at any time when over land. It was particularly useful in identifying the aiming point when the target was obscured by cloud, fog or smoke. Before the war ended, however, German scientists were able to adapt the equipment on Luftwaffe fighter planes, which enabled them to home on to any aircraft using

Left:
NAVIGATORS. Immediately ahead was the cabin where Graham Rose and Boris Bressloff, Navigator and 2nd Navigator/Radar Op respectively, sat facing the inside of the port fuselage at a table containing the charts, books and instruments of their trade. Flg Off P. Ingleby of No 619 Squadron is pictured at *his* 'desk' on 14 February 1944. *IWM CH12288*

57

'H2S'. As a result its use by Bomber Command was restricted to brief periods when over enemy territory, but the restriction did not apply to the target area if it was covered with cloud or smoke. For those who wondered why the new radar aid was given its name — they included the Thorne crew until Graham Rose enlightened them — 'H2S' is the scientific terminology for hydrogen sulphide, a particularly evil smelling gas. One member of the War Cabinet was very much against the introduction of the aid by Bomber Command. It had been reported that when he was asked to explain the reason for his opposition, he replied: 'It stinks! Call it H2S.'

A third device called 'Oboe' had been introduced in December 1941 and was used to great effect by two PFF Mosquito squadrons, operating with the Lancasters, to mark targets within a range of 350 miles. Don Bennett described Oboe as 'a very exact transmitter/responder system which could home an aircraft on a circular constant-radius distance to within an accuracy of 20ft or 30ft by transmitting a dash or dot signal. Another radius, cutting the first, was used to give the bomb release signal.' Two transmitters in England, one called 'Cat' transmitted dot or dash signals to the Mosquito pilot which told him if he

strayed off course. The bomb release signal came from another transmitter named 'Mouse'. It told the pilot when he was directly over the target and all he then had to do was press the button to release his TI or bombs. The Mosquitoes, flying at 30,000ft, did not carry defensive armament of any sort and Bennett was warned that their losses would be great. But the loss rate on the Mosquito squadrons turned out to be less than 1% per raid.

In the highly unlikely event of a malfunction of all these navigation aids, the navigators had to fall back on star-shots with a sextant which was part of their equipment. To keep in practice, the navigators took an opportunity to take their shots when safe to do so on the way home — and when the stars were visible, of course. The results were entered in their flight logs, and checked against the radar position as shown on Gee or H2S. Those taken by Gray and Boris were seldom in error when the comparison was made, which was more than could be said about Thorne's unofficial efforts at celestial navigation standing outside their billet, with less than polite urging from the others in the crew to pull his finger out; although on one memorable occasion his sextant reading placed them as being only a mere 100 miles from Downham Market!

The flight deck

Moving forward, Thorne and Parker came to their places in the cockpit. The pilot's seat was adjustable for height and leg space, and what at first seemed a maze of 67 instruments, dials, and controls stretched across the panels in front of him and to his left side. In the centre of the cockpit on his right side were the controls for the ailerons, flaps, elevators, rudders and undercarriage. Also by his right knee were the four engine throttle controls strategically placed to enable the flight engineer to assist in operating them on take-offs and landings as instructed by the pilot when he needed both hands on the flying controls.

On Thorne's right was a narrow gangway with a collapsible seat for flight engineer Harry Parker who, unlike the other members of the crew, had to do quite a lot of moving about. On his right, and slightly behind him, was a panel with about 20 dials, gauges and controls. They all required constant monitoring and there was a further array on the panel in front of him. All were important, but those which indicated the moment-to-moment performances of the four engines and their fuel consumption were vital. All Harry's actions and relevant observations during a flight had to be noted in his engineer's log. To add a spot of variety to his duties, it was his job also to unload, at precise intervals at set points over enemy territory, packets from a stack of parcels containing 'Window', the strips of foil which floated to earth causing chaos on the enemy's radar screens as they attempted to plot the size and direction of our attacking forces.

Behind Thorne and Parker, as they had been making their way up to the cockpit, came the remaining member of the crew to carry out his checks. Reg Keary, the bomb aimer, squeezed his way between them, through the cockpit and down the three narrow steps into his compartment with the dome-like perspex bowl at the front. On his left, as he lay on cushioned pads on the floor, was the computer into which he fed all the relevant data such as aircraft height, speed and drift expected on the run up to and over the target. From it ran two cables to the bomb-sight's gyro unit mounted on a thick flat panel of plate glass. Also on his

left, mounted on the floor, was a camera pre-set to act at the moment the aircraft's bombs exploded, while on his right were panels with 16 bomb release selection switches. In the roof of his compartment was the front gun turret with its two Browning guns. When he had completed all his arrangements and checks so far as bomb aiming was concerned, Keary could concentrate on his dual responsibilities as front gunner until the time came on the final leg of the outward trip when he would make the necessary adjustments in the computer for the attack on the target. Leaving his guns was a calculated and necessary risk because with the great closing speed of the Lancaster and an enemy fighter attacking head on, the situation rarely arose when he would be forced to open fire. On the other hand, when he was not immediately occupied with his vital task of ensuring that the bombs were released at exactly the right

time and on the right place — after all, that was the only reason for the Lancaster and its crew being there — his was another pair of eyes searching the outside for possible trouble.

By 11.00hrs, each man had completed his checks. As usual the groundcrew had done their work well and everything seemed to be on the top line. They were typical of the men who, at the mercy of the elements by day and by night, serviced their aircraft and kept them flying throughout the war. Their devotion to their work was sometimes taken for granted, but not by the aircrew and others directly concerned with the squadron's operations. After the war 'Bomber' Harris, speaking at one of the Pathfinder Association's Annual Dinners, paid tribute to the groundcrews of Bomber Command and deplored the fact that they had not been granted the official recognition he had recommended.

With the exception of Gray who, for a reason which now escapes one, wanted to go back to the navigation office, the rest of the crew voted for a quick coffee in Sly's Café before lunch. Mounting their bicycles, an essential form of transport for all ranks on a dispersed station, they all set off around the perimeter track and out on to the Bexwell Road for the one-mile ride into Downham Market. After parking their bikes against a wall by the Town Hall, they walked around the corner into Sly's shop with its inviting aromas of freshly baked bread and cakes, and through into the café at the rear of the premises. It was quite small, and the eight or nine tables were usually occupied by air-and-ground-crews who had been 'working late', enjoying a breakfast of Spam, chips and anything else available at the time such as sausages and even new-laid eggs from the local farm, all inevitably accompanied by tea or coffee and followed by hot toast and marmalade. The cost, if memory serves right, was half-a-crown (12½p in today's money). It was served by local ladies with maximum friendliness and minimum fuss. They seemed to know most of their customers by their first names. They never talked about anything connected with the squadron's activities, although at a reunion with them after the war they confessed how difficult it had been to conceal their feelings on many occasions when crews, to whom they had said cheerio as they left to return to the airfield, were never seen again.

In the middle of a friendly argument as to whose turn it was to pay the bill, Jack Catford, rear gunner in Wg Cdr Emile Mange's crew, came in. He took a spare chair from one of the tables, sat down next to Thorne and said: 'You're not on tonight; we are. And there are rumours of a daylight tomorrow.' The first part of Jack's communiqué was received with relief by the Thorne crew but when Reg Keary said quietly: 'I'll bet it's another Happy Valley tomorrow' there was just the nodding of heads in agreement. 'Let's get back' said Thorne. Boris insisted it was his turn to pay the bill and they left to collect their bicycles. There was no news when they arrived at the Mess so Boris and Thorne went into the bar. As they raised their glasses, Boris looked at Thorne and said: 'I'll bet you're thinking what I'm thinking'. Thorne knew he was referring to the target for tomorrow and he, too, had a feeling that he knew where it would be and that they would be on it. He just hoped they would be proved wrong so far as the first part of their prophesy was concerned.

Left:
Reg Keary, the bomb aimer, made his way down the three steps from the cockpit into his compartment with the dome-like perspex bowl at the front. Pictured here is the bomb aimer's nose position, complete with overhead twin Browning machine guns.

The hours before briefing

On leaving the Mess after lunch, Thorne and Boris cycled down to D-Dog to see if there was any information to be gleaned from the groundcrew on the petrol and bomb loads for the next day's op. The former would give them a pretty good idea of the distance, and the latter the type of target and their own role in the attack. It was a bright autumn day, and the Met forecast indicated a likely continuance of good weather over the next 24hr. But the groundcrew had no news to give them and, so far as they knew their colleagues on other dispersals were standing by, apart from those attached to aircraft taking part in the operation that night. Nothing had filtered through by 4 o'clock, which was understandable in view of the activities connected with the night op, so the two returned to their bikes and pedalled back along the perimeter to the billet. Gray had a pan of water on the stove (an upright contrivance with an iron pipe disappearing through the roof), so he put in some more water and found extra tea-leaves for the three of them.

They could be fairly sure it would not be an early take-off next day so they relaxed on their beds for an hour. Then Boris disappeared to go to the bath and shower hut 100yd away to find out if the water was running hot. He returned with a happy smile to confirm that it was near boiling point, so they picked up their towels and soap to ensure, as Gray said (and not for the first time) 'if they went for a Burton they would present a clean front to the Germans'.

'Gone for a Burton' was a phrase commonly used during the war by Air Force types to describe an unfortunate happening to someone. If so-and-so had been shot down, for instance, fallen off his bike or tripped over the Mess cat, he had 'Gone for a Burton'. The origin of the saying was never universally agreed upon but it is most likely to have been first used by would-be airmen on their wireless operators' course in Blackpool. They were tested at frequent intervals on their Morse transmitting and receiving speeds, and tests were carried out in the room over Burton's the tailors shop. If they failed in two consecutive tests they were likely to be taken off the course, so in the vernacular they had 'Gone for a Burton'.

Anyway, back to the bath and shower hut. There were six bathrooms: two were occupied and four did not have plugs, a state of affairs common to ablutions in all the Services. There were plenty of showers however, and by six o'clock the three D-Dog 'bods' (another Service play-around with the King's English) were on their way to the Mess and wondering if the battle order for tomorrow had been posted on the board. It was always Reg Keary who adopted a voice of doom when a target was revealed at briefing, with warnings such as 'It's the big chop tonight', or if it was not to be on the Ruhr or some other difficult area, 'It's when you're not expecting trouble that you get it'. It was a ritual for

Above:
The target-marking technique known as 'Wanganui' was named after the home town of Wg Cdr A. 'Artie' Ashworth DSO, DFC, AFC, a New Zealand-born leading member of No 635 Squadron (see p38).
Wg Cdr A. Ashworth DSO, DFC, AFC

the others in the crew to put on solemn faces and agree with him. It was a joke, and they would have thought there was something wrong with him if he had failed to put on this usual little act. They had a feeling though, that tomorrow it might not be a joke.

When they entered the Mess there was no one at the notice board, but there was a familiar oblong white paper pinned on the centre of the board and dated 6 October 1944. Eight crews were detailed for briefing at 10.30hrs. The Thorne crew was one of them. He went to the telephone in the Mess entrance hall and put a call through to the Sergeants' Mess. It brought Jim Raymont to the phone. He and the others had seen the battle order and it was then arranged that they should all meet at D-Dog's dispersal at 09.30hrs next morning. Although they had felt certain they would be on the battle order it was a relief to have it confirmed, so the three of them went into the bar and joined the few officers already in there.

The crews from the squadron who were on the operation that night had finished their pre-op meal of bacon and eggs and departed half-an-hour earlier for briefing, and it was not long before the bar customers started to drift off to the dining room for dinner. The place was unusually quiet, and after a leisurely meal the D-Dog trio started out on the 10min walk to the billet. There was little doubt in their minds that in around 20hr they would be over the Ruhr.

Cups of tea came to them next morning in the hands of Jimmy, the batman. There was usually a total of nine or 10 occupants of the hut, and apart from the Thorne trio whose home it was for 10 months until the end of the war, they were constantly changing for one reason or another. Looking back, the occasions seemed few and far between when they saw Jimmy at any time other than early in the morning. Yet the hut was always spick and span, beds made, uniforms pressed and laundry collected. All that must have taken some organising by Jimmy because with operations taking place by day and night he could never be sure when there would not be anyone asleep in there.

When the crews came together at the dispersal, an hour before they were due for briefing, the bomb doors beneath the fuselage were open, and looking up into the bomb bay they saw 18×500lb bombs; they were considered to be safe until fused by the fitting of a pistol containing mercury fulminate with a pin which would be withdrawn before take-off. But harmless though they may have been before they were released on the target by the bomb aimer, they always had a sinister look about them. The petrol bowser had been and gone, leaving 1,600gal in D-Dog's tanks. That usually indicated a round trip in the region of 500 miles, so with half-an-hour to briefing time it was back on to their bikes and around the perimeter track to the briefing room on the other side of the airfield to hear what the afternoon might have in store for them.

When they arrived there, Gray and Boris left the others to go into the navigation office to collect their maps and charts for the flight. The other crews were already filtering into the briefing room, having survived the searching looks of the two Service Police corporals at the door who were there to make sure there were no interlopers among them. The room had no windows and was about the size of an average village hall, say 70ft long by 30ft wide. Trestle tables and chairs were spread in two columns down its length. Each table was lettered with an aircraft identity and was to be occupied by the crew flying that aircraft. On the walls were drawings, charts and other works of art including contemporary Ministry of Information posters urging everyone to 'Be like Dad and keep Mum'. At the far end of the hall was the platform, at the back of which was a black curtain concealing a giant map of Europe. When the Station Commander and the squadron CO had arrived and taken their places, the show would begin with one of them pulling the curtain cord to reveal the target, with ribbons indicating the routes to be flown from base and back again. Permanent features on the map were the enemy's known flak defences illuminated in red, and the searchlight areas in blue. These usually were in two rings, the inner being the flak concentrations and the outer the searchlights. Large cities and important industrial targets naturally had the heaviest defence concentrations. The largest of all was the solid red and blue mass of colouring stretching on the map from Münster in the north down to below Cologne in the south — 100 miles by 70 at its widest point. A Happy Valley indeed!

The door opened at the rear of the hall and in came the navigators with their cases containing their documents for the flight. No sooner had they taken their seats than there was a clang as the door opened again and everyone stood as the Station Commander, Gp Capt W. H. ('Digger') Kyle* and Wg Cdr Sydney ('Tubby') Baker, the squadron CO, entered with the leaders of the various squadron sections: intelligence, met, navigation, gunnery, wireless, engineering, bombing and flying control. They all sat in front row seats except the Station Commander who said 'Please be seated' to the crews, stepped up on to the platform and pulled the cord to reveal the target, the sight of which was an anti-climax so far as most of the crews were concerned, and no one among the Thorne crew even said 'I told you so'. It was Gelsenkirchen.

Having completed his unveiling of the map showing the target and the routes to and from it, the Station Commander stepped down and the CO took his place. Pointing to the battle order displayed at the side of the map showing the crews' names, he asked the captains if all their crews were present. Each captain

*Later ACM Sir Wallace Kyle GCB, KCVO, CBE, DSO, DFC

Above:
Wg Cdr S. 'Tubby' Baker DSO, DFC and Bar, OC No 635 Squadron PFF, who completed 100 operational sorties. *IWM CH16198*

answered in the affirmative, so pointing to the map he continued:

'This is a familiar sight to all of you. We know that the previous attacks have severely damaged the synthetic oil plants in the area but the production, although significantly reduced, continues. Every

gallon of oil is vital to the enemy to continue the war so it is even more vital that we should stop them. Two separate attacks will be made this afternoon, one on the Scholven/Buer plant at 16.55-17.05hrs, the other at 17.06-17.18hrs on the Sterkrade/Holten plant. You will be on the first attack, taking off at 15.00hrs. Twenty-three Lancasters and 10 Mosquitoes from PFF Group will lead a Main Force of 128 Halifaxes from No 4 Group. The same numbers of PFF Group Lancasters and Mosquitoes will lead 126 Halifaxes from No 4 Group on Sterkrade/Holten. Twelve Spitfire and four Mustang squadrons will give fighter cover from the Dutch coast to the target. At the end of the attacks they will disperse to shepherd their respective bomber streams.'

That was all the CO had to say for the time being, and his place was taken by the Intelligence Officer. 'Gelsenkirchen', he said, 'is one of the greatest industrial centres in the world'. And as an afterthought he added that it was reputed to have the two best horse-racing tracks in Europe. After giving additional emphasis to 'Tubby' Baker's comments regarding the enemy being able to produce sufficient supplies of synthetic oil to continue the war, he had some disturbing information relevant to the coming operation. The route to the target would be as short as possible 'in the interests of efficient fighter cover'. Most of it would be just behind the German battlefront where flak had been greatly increased and where sightings of

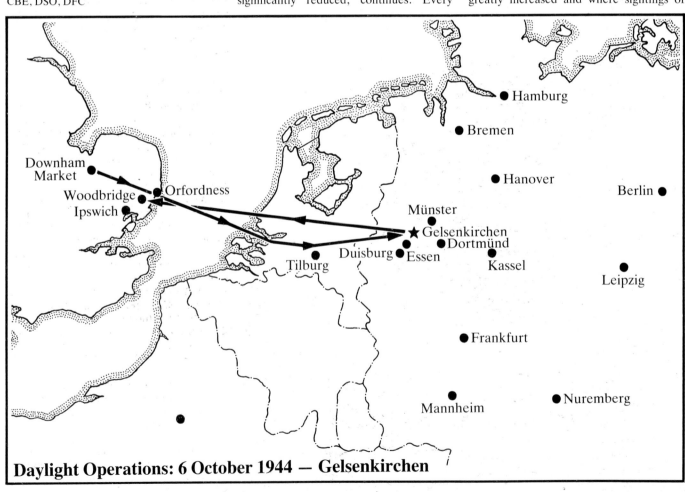

Daylight Operations: 6 October 1944 — Gelsenkirchen

62

jet-propelled aircraft had been reported. The flak had been heavy enough in previous Gelsenkirchen operations, and to learn that it had been greatly increased was bad news, but the reference to jet fighters was of particular interest to D-Dog's crew.

During a night operation on Kiel on 15 September, Thorne and Harry Parker had seen a streak of flame rising at great speed high above them on the starboard side. As they were approaching the target at the time, they did not let it distract their attention from the immediate objective, but Thorne had reported the sighting at debriefing on return to base. No one seemed very interested at the time, but following the Gelsenkirchen raid three weeks later, a Bomber Command report referred to jet-propelled aircraft having been sighted by a bomber. The Thorne crew did not see any jets after the one at Kiel although it was known that the USAAF in their formations had suffered considerable losses from the new menace.

The Intelligence Officer continued: 'From what I've just said, you will gather that flak will be your principal worry. We don't think there will be much trouble from fighters, certainly not in the vicinity of the

Below:
WO Jimmy Huck RCAF, a tail gunner with No 61 Squadron, who was one of the first to shoot down a Messerschmitt Me262 jet fighter.

target for obvious reasons.' By that he meant that the barrage would be as dangerous for them as it would be for the attacking force. After the usual reminders on escape procedures for anyone being forced down on the wrong side of the German front – 'bury your parachute, hide until darkness comes then head for what could be a comparatively short distance to the Allied lines; empty your pockets before you leave this room, and captains make sure that each member of your crew has his escape aids' – the Intelligence Officer gave way to the Met Officer. His forecast was short in delivery. 'Good weather conditions over the routes and targets, which means clear skies to provide good targets for the flak defences'. That prompted Reg to comment that they couldn't have it all ways, a surprisingly mild statement coming from the usual prophet of doom.

During the briefing the navigators had been working hard on the finishing touches to their charts which they had started to compile during their short period in the navigation room before the main briefing commenced. At the same time they had kept an ear open to everything the CO and Intelligence Officer had said, and to the short but succinct forecast from the Met Officer. It was now the Navigation Officer's turn to continue the main briefing for all the assembled aircrews. With pointer in hand he traced the route to be taken from base, first to Orfordness where the Master Bomber and his Deputy with their Supporters should be just ahead of the Main Force, with the Visual Centrers

spaced according to the timings as planned. Spot-on PFF timing would, as always, be of the utmost importance with 161 aircraft scheduled to be in and out of the target area within a time space of 10min. The Thorne crew, making what they expected would be their penultimate trip as a Supporter, would go in with the Master Bomber at 16.55hrs at a height of 16,000ft.

From Orfordness, the red lines on the map stretched from base to the Scheldt Estuary with its slim-looking islands, which Jim Raymont always referred to as 'the beckoning fingers'. From there a change of course to the north skirting Tilburg was calculated to indicate to the enemy an attack on Essen, Duisberg or Dortmund; but after another change of course to the north the route pointed north of Essen, to Gelsenkirchen. As the CO had said, it was only too familiar to the Lancaster crews, and the same would probably apply to the majority in Main Force. On leaving the target, all aircraft were to make a sharp turn north on to what was nearly a reciprocal course and head for home.

The Gunnery Leader had his usual little sermon for the gunners. 'Keep your guns and eyes moving all the time. Give your pilots plenty of warning of the positions and movements of any fighters but do not open fire unless you believe your aircraft is directly threatened. Also keep your pilot informed of anything else happening within your range of vision which you think may help keep him informed of the running situation. You are all experienced so there is no need for me to warn you of the danger of both gunners concentrating on one fighter which may threaten you whilst another is coming in to attack from another quarter.'

It was then the turn of the Wireless Officer, or Radio Officer as he became more suitably titled after the war, to run through the duties of his operators; there was always plenty for them to do from take-off to landing – apart from controlling the aircraft's internal heating! For example, they listened out for Group broadcasts every 10min past and 20min to every hour. If there was no message they would transmit a number, different each time, which the W/Op had to log to confirm that he had been receiving. When over enemy territory, Group HQ would locate the frequency on which the German fighter controller was broadcasting and pass it on to the W/Op. He would then pick up the German R/T and switch on carbon microphones attached to the brushes on the aircraft's generators, then back-tune his transmitter and press his Morse key. The unholy row this produced in the ears of the German fighter controller can be imagined, and it remained thus until he had gone through the business of changing his transmitter frequency, when the whole procedure began again.

Another duty was to transmit wind changes to Group. Such changes were calculated by the navigator and passed to the W/Op. When Group received the

information they quickly determined the mean average change and passed it to all aircraft on the raid, thus helping all of them to keep on track. There was one other task the members of the crew always made sure the W/Op had carried out, not that he would have been likely to forget it for his own safety. He had to make sure that the photo-flash had gone with the bombs when they were released. It was fused to ignite at 1,000ft and if it had remained stuck for any reason, the result when the aircraft descended to that height can be imagined.

The Station Flying Control Officer was the last of the Section Officers to say his piece. Pointing to the captains' names on the battle order list at the side of the map, he began: 'This will be the order for take-off starting with D-Dog at 13.17hrs on the long runway, east to west. Call Base Control as you cross the coast on your return, giving simply the Station call-sign and your aircraft identity.' RAF Downham Market call-sign was 'Offstrike'; No 635 Squadron's aircraft call-sign was 'Cut-out' followed by the identity of the particular aircraft (thus Thorne would call 'Offstrike from Cut-out D-Dog'). 'Approach the circuit at 2,000ft, or below cloud if there is any, call Control and then follow instructions. Call again when you are down to 1,000ft, switch on your identity lights, prepare to land and call again as you enter the funnel giving simply your aircraft identity. If the runway is clear you will be told to land, if it is not clear you will be told to go round again.' (The 'funnel' was when one was in line with, and descending on to, the runway.) He concluded: 'Turn right at the end of the runway and on to your dispersal point.'

The CO asked finally if there were any questions. There was none. 'Transport is outside to take you to your Messes for your meal. See you later!' As he left the briefing room, everyone stood up: there was a loud scraping of chairs, stretching of arms and legs (the aircrews' not the chairs') and collecting of maps, charts, logs and notes made during the briefing. But before they moved to the doors there were two routines for the aircrew to carry out.

A couple of WAAFs came in carrying small canvas bags into which the crew members placed anything they had in their pockets which might be of use to German Intelligence in the event of an aircraft crashing on enemy territory, with survivors – if any – being subjected to interrogation. This may seem to be a superfluous exercise because all aircrew had been indoctrinated with the need for care in such details, and the vital importance of providing their interrogators with only their name and service number if they were captured.

They had been given examples of the sort of situation they might come up against and one of them concerned a member of a Stirling crew who had landed safely by parachute when his aircraft was shot down near Essen. He was picked up and taken to the local police station where they took his jacket from him and he was left alone for three days. He was eventually taken to a room where a smiling German officer greeted him by name, invited him to sit down, offered him a cigarette and said: 'You've had a bit of hard luck haven't you! Never mind, you're safe now, although I'm afraid it may be some time before you dance again in the Locarno.'

That was a bit of a shaker for the prisoner. He lived at Streatham in South-east London and he enjoyed the occasional evening in that popular ballroom when he was on leave. In fact he had taken his girlfriend there during his last leave. The interpreter let a few seconds elapse to note the prisoner's surprised reaction to his captor's knowledge of even a minor happening in his private life. Then he suddenly said: 'Right, that's all for now. I'll see you later.'

Strangely, neither of them saw each other again because within a few days the airman was posted to a permanent POW camp from which he escaped some months later and made his way back to England. Here, as with all other escapees, he went through another period of questioning, this time from RAF interrogators. They seemed only mildly interested when he told them about the ballroom reference. One of them asked:

'Did you get tickets when you went to the Locarno?'
'Yes' he replied.
'Do you remember where you put the counterfoils?'
He thought for a while and answered: 'I suppose I put them in my pocket.'
'Which pocket?'
'I think in the top right pocket.'
'What sort of tickets were they: card or paper?'
'Well, the counterfoils were just small slips of paper.'
'I'm sure the odds are that they found them in your pocket.'
'But what good would it do them?'
'It worried you didn't it, and you probably spent a long time thinking over what else they might know. It was the first step in trying to make you think how clever they were and eventually creating a frame of mind in which you might believe it was useless trying to avoid answering further questions which at first would seem innocuous enough. Then they would proceed into more exact details about your squadron, personnel, aircraft and goodness knows what else. It's the usual technique. But then, we don't know for certain that they did find a ticket counterfoil in your pocket. You'll be going back to your squadron so don't worry about it.'

That's the story told by one of the intelligence lecturers at RAF Rufforth and it must have been a stock performance by other lecturers on the subject of interrogation procedures because everyone in Bomber Command seemed to have heard it. And it was certainly apocryphal because it was unlikely that a gunner would be wearing his uniform jacket on an op, and just as unlikely that he would wear his battledress jacket in a public ballroom. Nevertheless, true or fictional, the story had the desired effect and there were few among aircrew who did not give a last-minute dip in the corners of their pockets before the WAAFs sealed each canvas bag and took them away for the return of the contents, if any, to the owners at the debriefing.

While the emptying of pockets was going on, Thorne had handed out escape aids to the D-Dog crew. Each of the aids was contained in a neat little package about the size of a flat 50-cigarette tin. One packet contained concentrated glucose and chocolate, condensed milk in a tube, benzedrine pep tablets, water purifying tablets, matches, fishing line and hook, safety razor, toothbrush, compass, a small leather water bottle and soap. There was also a purse containing currency of the countries over which they would fly. In another purse was a silk handkerchief on which were printed maps of the countries on the route. Everyone also carried a personal first-aid kit which supplemented the larger kits carried on the aircraft. It contained dressings, an ampoule of morphia with syringe, burn jelly and a pair of specially treated gloves for wearing over badly burned hands, one of the most common injuries suffered by aircrew. Then came an ingenious collection of 'secret' compasses concealed in RAF uniform buttons or on fountain pens. Or two trouser buttons, one of which had to be balanced on top of the other – it then swung round and pointed to magnetic north. Perhaps the cleverest was the compass concealed in a briar pipe. It could be smoked in the normal way but when the mouth-piece was unscrewed a small section could be separated from the middle of the stem to reveal a tiny compass. All clever stuff and live-savers on many occasions.

According to the time of take-off the 'operational meal' was served either before or after briefing and it was usually enjoyed more in the latter instance, maybe because it is human nature to be more relaxed when one knows what the immediate future holds, even if it may be a trip to the Ruhr, rather than having the additional worry of uncertainty. Anyway, thoughts of another visit to Gelsenkirchen did not seem to affect the appetites of the crews concerned and there were no signs of despondency as they boarded the transports which had been waiting to carry them to their locker rooms in the Flight hut where they would collect their flying clothing and parachutes. The weather remained fine and clear and warm for the time of year, so apart from the gunners there was no particular

Left:
KRIEGIE. Sgt Dennis Merrills, air gunner and ex-Halton aircraft apprentice, being interrogated after landing in Germany; the beginning of long weary years as a prisoner of war. *IWM GER1025*

dressing up to be done. Within an hour the six crews of 635 Squadron were climbing back into the transport vehicles to be driven to their respective dispersals. D-Dog's groundcrew were waiting by the aircraft and reported that all was OK, the starter trolley with its battery of accumulators stood near the port side front wheel ready to be plugged in and, with just over one hour to go before take-off, the crew climbed the steel ladder to enter the fuselage. They were: Alex Thorne (Pilot), Graham Rose (Navigator), Boris Bressloff (2nd Nav and Radar Operator), Jim Crabtree (Wireless Operator), Harry Parker (Flight Engineer), Reg Keary (Bomb Aimer), Jim Raymont (Rear Gunner), and Jock Scott (Mid-Upper Gunner).

They settled down and prepared to run through their pre-take-off checks which had become a matter of routine since their first flight in a Lancaster with Wg Cdr Rodley three months previously. Once everyone was settled in his seat headphones were put on and they waited for the engines to be started. 'Contact!' Thorne shouted to the starter trolley crew. The lead was connected to the port inner engine, then it was the ground operator's turn to shout 'Contact!' in reply, and the first engine began to turn, hesitantly at first, before bursting into life. When all the engines had been started, Thorne opened each up slowly, adjusted the throttle controls to synchronise them at 1,200rpm and kept them there until they had warmed up sufficiently for Harry to check temperatures and pressures and test the operation of the hydraulic system by lowering and raising the wing flaps. That was also the time for the bomb doors to be closed hydraulically on the 18 × 500lb bombs. They would not be opened again, except in an emergency, until Reg Keary called for Harry to operate the lever in the cockpit which would open them at the critical moment approaching the target.

When the crew had completed their tests they called Thorne on the intercom. No one had any snags to report and as there remained half-an-hour before take-off they left their leather flying helmets and headphones on the seats and made their way down to the ground for a final breath of fresh air and a stretch. The ground sergeant handed Thorne the Form 700 to sign, confirming that the regulation pre-flight checks had been carried out and that, in his opinion, the aircraft was serviceable. One last cigarette for those who used them — all the groundcrew did but half the aircrew didn't — and it was back up the ladder again with five minutes remaining before take-off at 15.00hrs. Engines were started again and at a wave from Thorne and thumbs up from the groundcrew the chocks were removed and D-Dog was on its way. During the trundle along the perimeter track towards the long east-west runway, He double-checked that the ground/flight switch was at 'FLIGHT' and the radiator shutter switches were 'OPEN', while Thorne confirmed to the navigators that his altimeter was set to take account of the airfield's height above sea level. The black and white chequered caravan and its crew — 'the runway traffic wardens' — with their signals equipment including red and green torches, could be seen waiting at the end of the runway. From his rear turret Jim Raymont reported over the intercom that there were four aircraft following behind them. There was also one ahead of D-Dog and as it turned right off of the perimeter and along the concrete track towards the caravan it was identified as S-Sugar. As usual, there was a line of people near the caravan who had come to watch the take-off. Among them was Margaret, one of the squadron intelligence officers, who had always endeavoured to be there to join the others in waving the crews on their way, a kindly gesture which was always appreciated.

Below:
Ready for take-off.

Right:
When all engines had been started, Harry opened each up slowly and adjusted the throttle controls to synchronise them at 1,200rpm. *IWM CH11912*

Below right:
At a wave from Thorne and thumbs up from the groundcrew the chocks were removed and 'D-Dog' was on its way.
P. G. Davys via A. Thomas

D-Dog was brought to a stop at a right-angle to the runway. Thorne and Harry Parker made a quick double-check on the trimming tabs (elevators slightly forward, rudders and ailerons neutral, flaps 20° down). He confirmed that fuel cocks and booster pumps were OK. A green light came from outside the caravan. S-Sugar moved forward on to the runway, stopped and waited for a second green light for the take-off. It came quickly and with an increasing roar from the engines they were on their way. As soon as S-Sugar began its lift-off the green light came on for D-Dog to move on to the runway. Thorne

opened the throttles slowly and the green light came on immediately. The throttles were opened to zero boost to test against the brakes to ensure the engines responded evenly. Then he throttled back, released the brakes and reopened the throttles, checking the tendency to swing to port by advancing the port throttles slightly ahead of those on the starboard side. Harry had his left hand behind Thorne's right hand and as the aircraft gained forward momentum he called out the speeds: '80-90-95-100'. Thorne eased the control column forward, and, as the tail lifted, the aircraft became lighter to control. 'Yours, Harry' he said as he moved his hand off the throttle and on to the control column making sure that Harry had taken over to continue increasing the engines' revs. At 110mph, when they were three-quarters of the way up the runway and at full power, Thorne eased back the control column, the nose lifted and they were airborne.

He throttled back about a quarter and called 'Wheels up'. Harry pulled back the undercarriage control lever, there was a rumbling vibration beneath them followed

by a click. 'Wheels up and locked', said Harry. At 500ft the flaps were raised causing a nose down change of trim. Harry switched off the electric fuel booster pumps of Nos 1 and 2 tanks. Thorne set a climbing speed of 160mph and began a turn to port towards their first turning point at Orfordness. When they reached 9,000ft he called 'Oxygen on, everybody'.

It was mandatory for that to be done at no greater height than 10,000ft. Mental deterioration caused by oxygen starvation usually started at around 14,000ft, depending upon the individual. It became steadily worse above that height with the victim becoming increasingly unaware of his erratic behaviour. The oxygen itself came through a rubber tube and into the oxygen mask, fitted over the airman's nose and mouth and held in place by press studs on each side of his flying helmet. When the switch on the mask was moved to the 'ON' position the user could test for the oxygen coming through by holding the mask very slightly away from his face. If he could feel what seemed like very gentle puffs of air on his lips they would, in fact, be puffs of

Below:
The throttles were open to zero boost to test against the brakes, then Thorne throttled back, released the brakes and reopened the throttles. *IWM CH14188*

Below right:
As the aircraft gained forward momentum, Harry called out the speeds: '80-90-95-100. *IWM CH10675*

Right:
Thorne eased back the control column and they were airborne. Harry pulled back the undercarriage control lever; there was a rumbling vibration beneath them followed by a click: wheels up and locked.

oxygen. They would not be felt when the mask was fitted back on to his face. It was really very simple although rather complicated to explain.

During the first leg, the Lancasters from the other PFF squadrons participating in the operation had joined the No 635 Squadron aircraft and together they all turned on to the new course towards the next turning point on the Dutch mainland east of Schouwen. As they approached the enemy coast at a height of 16,000ft the Halifaxes of Main Force came in behind them. From their No 4 Group bases in Yorkshire they had been converging on the Lancasters which, of course, had crossed the English coast at a more southerly point. Ten minutes before reaching the Dutch coast Gray had told Thorne that they were 'bang on time and that he would give him the new heading five minutes before they had to turn'. There were only a few degrees to turn to the north when he came through again: 'OK Skipper, turn now. Next turning point is at our old friend Tilburg.'

He had hardly had time to switch off from his short transmission when the first flak bursts appeared around D-Dog and the other front-flying aircraft. They were all well predicted and at about the same height as the leading Lancasters, all of which pressed on, the pilots knowing that no good was likely to result from deviating in their flight. There was no sign of any fighter opposition but the flak was now spreading in a wide band ahead of them. There came a click in Thorne's headphones as one of the crew switched on. It was Jim in the rear turret: 'Heavy flak behind us. Two Hallies have just collided about two miles back and they're going down. What's it like ahead?'

'It's pretty busy but I can see Tilburg so we're well on our way' Thorne replied. The now familiar chimneys and factory buildings were indeed in sight. Thorne switched on his intercom and was about to ask Gray how long before the next change of course when there was a heavy thump. D-Dog rolled over to starboard and the port inner engine started racing as if it wanted to get

the hell out of the mess by itself. He immediately pulled back its throttle; the aircraft wallowed and started to roll to port with the loss of power on that side. He throttled back the starboard inner engine to equalise the pull as far as possible and regained a measure of stability and control. By that time they had lost height and were down to 10,000ft, and still losing height, so he started juggling with the revs, advancing those of the port outer engine until, he hoped, the aircraft would maintain height. At 2,600rpm D-Dog settled at level flight but they were now down to 8,000ft, a state of affairs to which the ground batteries responded with obvious, and understandable, delight.

While all this was going on — and it did not take much longer than it did to describe it — Gray's voice came on the intercom: 'Boris has been hit, Skipper'.
Thorne: 'Tell me more.'
Boris: 'It's OK, something hit me in the back but I'm OK — I think.'
Gray: 'I'm just pulling off his 'chute harness and Mae West.'

Going over.

Thorne: 'Let me know.'

Two minutes later: 'Boris here. Yes everything's OK. I felt a bang in my back and my Mae West is split right down. Not a tear in my jacket though. Extraordinary. A piece of flak I suppose.'

Thorne: 'That's good. You must be more careful next time. Cheers!'

They were then just passing Tilburg down on the starboard side. Both inner engines were still throttled right back and as Thorne started to advance them slowly, with some trepidation so far as the port inner was concerned, Harry's voice came over the intercom:

'Gray — Harry here; thought you'd like to know we're just passing Tilburg, starboard side.'

Gray: 'Yes, thanks Harry . . . Alex, turn on to 080 degrees. Target 85 miles on.'

Thorne confirmed the change of course, reset his compass and continued increasing the inner engine's revs. The previous course had been heading toward Essen, but any hope that the enemy would have been fooled into believing this was to be the target area was dispelled when the barrage from the ground guns became even more intense and accurate as the Lancasters and Halifaxes changed direction and headed for Gelsenkirchen. Jock Scott in the mid-upper turret reported two more Halifaxes down on the port side. Meanwhile, to Thorne's surprise and relief, the port inner engine had withstood an increase of power up to 1,200rpm in step with the starboard engine, at which point it began to vibrate. It was sufficient, though, to maintain the aircraft's height at 8,000ft so they pressed on towards the target.

Above:
During the first leg, the Lancasters of other PFF squadrons participating in the operation joined us. *IWM CH18684*

Harry had been keeping a close watch on the fuel situation and reported no signs of loss from the port inner, but he was ready to feather the propeller and switch off if the engine seized up. At 16.30hrs Boris called Thorne: 'After all that we're only three minutes behind schedule. Can you step on it a bit?.' 'We'll try,' Thorne replied. There were now four Lancasters and eight or nine Halifaxes ahead, he assumed two of the Lancs would be the Master Bomber and his Deputy. The gunners reported 'a flock of Halifaxes' close behind stretching back up to two miles at around 16,000ft and ploughing their way, said Jock Scott, through the flak. D-Dog, down at 8,000ft, was attracting a lot of light flak as well as the heavy stuff.

Thorne had been on the point of increasing the revs on the outer engines to obtain more height but to do so would have meant falling further behind in their time on target. He chose to concentrate first on gaining more speed by increasing the outer engines to 2,850rpm which they should have been able to stand for up to one hour. The port engine had been running at 1,200rpm for about five minutes. Would it take more now? Thorne told Harry what he proposed to do; Harry put his thumbs up, and the two inner throttles were slowly advanced. The few minutes' comparative rest for the port inner must have had some

Left:
MID-UPPER. The all-round panorama of sky available to a dorsal gunner — an infinity of space which might at any moment 'disgorge' an attacking enemy fighter.

75

recuperative effect on whatever ailed it, caused by the hit at Tilburg, but it jibbed on 1,450rpm at which point the vibrations started again. Thorne throttled it back to 1,400rpm but continued increasing the starboard inner, compensating for the aircraft's resultant pull to port by exerting extra pressure with his right leg on the rudder control. Within a minute D-Dog had touched 200mph and as they were nearing the run-up to the target Thorne decided to abandon any thought of gaining height at the expense of extra speed in an effort to make up for lost time. Harry would give Reg Keary all the data he required for his bomb release calculations while he, Thorne, would concentrate on getting as much out of the engines as was possible. Visibility remained excellent, apart from the clouds of black stuff from the exploding shells which hung in the air on all quarters from around 7,000ft up to and above the Main Force at 16,000ft. The two gunners, Jim and Jock, reported several instances of aircraft making sudden violent movements off their course – an indication that they had been hit by flak – but they had not seen any go down since the four already reported. Official reports following the two attacks on the Gelsenkirchen targets that afternoon stated that 70% of the aircraft had been hit by flak.

So far, enemy fighters had been conspicuous by their absence which was understandable in view of the concentrated and continuous gunfire from the ground defences. D-Dog remained uncomplaining at 200mph and was slowly closing on the leading Lancs; Harry was busy keeping an eagle eye on his gauges and scribbling in his log. Reg was performing on his bombing computers, and Thorne's right leg was going numb. Boris came on the intercom: 'You should see the Mossie TIs in about ten minutes'. Reg stretched out on his cushion ready for the bombing run. They were still, Thorne reckoned, about two minutes behind the leaders which was not bad in the circumstances – providing their luck, since leaving Tilburg, held. Then down came the first Mosquito TI, bursting in a flash of yellow and shimmering on the ground. Every Master Bomber (MB) in PFF had his own call-sign, also

Above left:
Halifax BIII, MZ759, NP-Q of No 158 Squadron hit by flak and on fire over Gladbeck (Ruhr) crashed within minutes of this photograph, taken from Lancaster S-Sugar of No 408 Squadron RCAF on 24 March 1945.

Left:
A night scene above Dusseldorf on 10/11 September 1942 showing tracer, flak and searchlight trails. *IWM C3128*

Above right:
Cologne, as seen from 17,500ft at 10.02hrs on 2 May 1945 by Flg Off Huddon in Lancaster U-Uncle of No 170 Squadron.

Right:
Hanover 'all lit up' on 22 October 1943. *IWM C3898*

used by his Deputy (DMB). On this attack the Pathfinders and Main Force carried red TIs. The MB, following closely behind his DMB, had to do three things at once – follow his bomb aimer's instructions during the run-up, assess the accuracy of the TIs already on the ground, and broadcast his instructions to the Main Force following. His voice came loud and clear, repeating twice: 'Skylark One to Main Force. Bomb the red TIs.'

D-Dog was still alone at 8,000ft and when a Halifax at 16,000ft was hit by flak and went spiralling down on the starboard side, a bit too close for Thorne's peace of mind, Reg Keary started his instructions on the intercom: 'Bomb doors open, Skip.'

Thorne: 'Bomb doors open.'

Reg: 'Right a bit . . . Hold that . . . Steady . . . right a bit.'

(Thorne's right leg was stiffened against the pull to port).

Reg: 'That's fine, coming up nicely . . . Steady . . . Steady . . . Bombs gone!' D-Dog's nose lifted. 'Bomb doors closed.'

A straight course had to be held for at least 30sec for the photo-flash to go off. It was a nerve-wracking time for every aircrew but D-Dog was bearing a charmed life. At last Gray's voice came over: 'Hard left, Skipper, on to two-nine-zero'. It was almost a reciprocal course and as they turned they could see the Halifaxes

streaming into the attack and the TIs and bombs bursting on the target. Thorne was about to ask Harry the state of the engines and fuel when there came a loud bang as though a giant fist had punched the port wing. Looking down Thorne could see flames streaming back from the port inner engine. He pulled back the throttles of both inner engines, banged Harry on the arm and pointed downwards though the port window. Harry stood up to look across him, saw what was happening, swung around to his instrument panel, turned off the fuel cock to the engine, pressed the fire extinguisher and feathering buttons on his flight engineer's instrument panel, and completed the performance by switching off the engine. Thorne then started to advance the starboard inner engine revs and now that speed was not a vital requirement he reduced the two outer engines' revs until D-Dog was flying at 175mph.

The 'charmed life' period had lasted no longer than half-an-hour, but they were still the target for heavy and light flak. Thorne could not risk increasing power to gain height until he was assured of adequate fuel remaining after the comparatively heavy consumption to increase speed following the first hit, and then the loss of fuel from the now silent and flame-free port inner. While Harry was working on the fuel state Thorne switched on his intercom:

'Hello there, Alex here. Starting from the rear turret will you tell me if you are all OK and then I'll tell you what the situation is. Over.' The replies came in quick order from everyone 'All OK Skipper'.

Thorne: 'We've had to feather the port inner but we're going well on three engines and I'll try to increase height.' He did not tell them about the fire.

The attack on the target must have gone according to plan because the MB's instructions to Main Force which, of course, had been received by D-Dog, had not varied from 'Bomb the reds' or 'Overshoot the reds by five seconds. Don't creep back.' As the raid progressed it was not unusual for the bombing to creep back from the aiming point, but the MB invariably recognised the tendency and corrected it immediately. Five minutes after Reg Keary had released D-Dog's bombs the MB's voice came over for the last time on this trip: 'Skylark One to Main Force. I'm going home now. That was a good show. Have good trip, and thank you.'

When Harry came back with his verdict on the remaining fuel it could have been better. Briefly, if there was no further trouble D-Dog would make base but he would be monitoring the consumption at the present speed and height. If the margin looked too fine it would be wise to land at Woodbridge, the emergency landing airfield 12 miles northeast of Ipswich, and 10 miles inside the Suffolk coast. 'How far to

Below:
This picture of the aircrews of No 635 Squadron was taken a week after VE day. Graham Rose and Boris Bressloff are third and fourth on the second row right. The other members of the Thorne crew returned on the following day — apart from Thorne who was languishing in bed at home with chickenpox.

the Dutch coast?' Thorne asked Gray. Within a few seconds Grey came back: 'One hundred and twenty miles'.

The next half-an-hour passed slowly although the flak had certainly become more erratic, with the enemy gun batteries seemingly undecided whether to concentrate on predicated aim or a barrage. The comparatively low-flying D-Dog was apparently being ignored after half the distance to the coast had been covered and the ultimate sight of the islands in the Scheldt Estuary – Jim's 'beckoning fingers' – were a welcome sight. What was not so welcome was the fuel consumption which surged up and down at intervals for no apparent reason. Then as the coastal islands loomed ever nearer, so did the suddenly increasing flak bursts around them. There were odd 'pings' as spent light flak hit the fuselage but D-Dog pressed on. Another five minutes and they would be over Walcheren and leaving the guns behind them.

But it did not work out that way. As Thorne's view of the islands slipped away under D-Dog's nose, the port outer engine began to lose power and there was a startling thump from the rear of the aircraft with a simultaneous violent downward swerve to port. It was corrected by a quick pull back of the starboard outer engine revs but a lot of height had been lost by the time Thorne regained a semblance of control. Although the height was checked at 3,000ft it was difficult to control

direction, the reason for which came from Jock Scott in the mid-upper turret: 'Jock here, Skipper. The port rudder's gone.'

Thorne to Jock: 'That's all we need. Never mind, we're over the sea so we can soon sort things out in peace.'

Thorne to Jim Raymont: 'Are you OK and did you hear what Jock's just said?'

Jim: 'Yes, he got in before me. In fact the remains of the starboard rudder are hanging down below the tail plane. Jock probably can't see it from his position.'

Thorne: 'Thanks Jim. Will you others come on and tell me if you're OK.' An affirmative came from each.

Thorne to Gray: 'I'm trying to hold height at 3,000ft with the two starboard engines but I'm going to land at Woodbridge. Will you give me the course, please?'

There were two reasons why he had abandoned any thoughts of heading for base. Harry was worried over the fuel situation and Thorne himself was finding it a struggle to keep anything approaching a straight heading with one rudder and only two engines, both of them on the same side causing a load on his right leg even heavier than before. Reg Keary came up from his

bomb aiming position to try to take some of the load by half sitting at Thorne's side and bracing his left leg on the rudder control, but there was not enough back support for him to maintain any appreciable pressure. In any case height was being lost, although slowly, and Thorne decided to at least prepare for a possible ditching. Gray had replied to his earlier request for a course to Woodbridge and Thorne made a dual call on the intercom:

'Alex here to Gray and Jim (Radio): Will you, Gray, give Jim our position, height, speed etc, and then you, Jim, send out a Mayday call. Let me know when that's done and we'll then prepare for a possible ditching. This is just to be on the safe side. Harry says our fuel will be OK but we must be sure we can maintain sufficient height to reach Woodbridge.'

Within a couple of minutes Jim came back: 'Jim (Radio) to Alex. Mayday accepted. Everything in hand, they have us covered. I have to contact them every five

minutes or less if necessary.'

Ten minutes later D-Dog was down to 2,500ft. Harry said: 'OK, Alex. Fuel crossfeed to starboard engine's OK. At this rate we'll make Woodbridge.'

Thorne put up his thumb to Harry and called Gray and Jim again: 'You heard Harry then, we'll press on as we are and if things still look good you can cancel the Mayday at the end of 10 minutes.'

At 18.00hrs the Suffolk coast could be seen ahead. Jim had cancelled the Mayday, Harry was confident that the fuel would get them to Woodbridge and Jim Raymont and Jock had moved from their turrets to crash positions in the fuselage. The three push-out panels in the fuselage roof had been loosened to be ready in case of a crash landing, Boris said his 'Gee' box told him they were on course, and Thorne wondered what it would be like to land at Woodbridge with its runway 3,000yd long and 250yd wide. During the war 4,120 aircraft in distress had landed there including a Junkers-88 whose German pilot heaved a sigh of relief when he landed safely one foggy night in July 1944 with the help of the Woodbridge FIDO installation. He thought he was in German-occupied Holland.

D-Dog's height had been reduced gradually to 1,000ft as the coast was reached. Thorne was prepared for a two-engined landing hoping that it would not be too rough with only one rudder and half its engines. He also had in mind the undercarriage – had it been damaged? He would never know. At what he believed was a height of around 500ft, with a runway lined up nicely ahead, the starboard inner engine cut out. With only one engine still working D-Dog swerved to port in a despairing dive. He quickly pulled back the throttle, D-Dog righted itself, forced its way through a line of saplings, bumped on a line of rising ground beyond and miraculously came to rest in a field on the other side of the rise. A few seconds of silence was broken by a minor explosion on the port wing, Harry pulled out the escape panel from the cockpit roof, climbed out on to the starboard wing and turned to help out Reg. Thorne looked down the fuselage although he could not see anyone, so he followed the other two. As they jumped from the wing on to the ground there was a sound of exploding ammunition from the rear of the fuselage and the crackling of fire around the port wing. They could see Gray, Boris, Jim Raymont and Jock. It took a few seconds for them to realise that Jim Crabtree was missing. A frantic search failed to find him and D-Dog was now burning furiously. It was not until later that evening that a RAF rescue team from Woodbridge found his body beneath the charred remains of the aircraft. It would have been impossible for Gray or Boris to go past his seat and down the fuselage as they did without seeing him. The reason for his death remains a mystery.

The next thing Thorne remembers is waking up in a wood to which the crew had taken him on the boundary of the field

where they had crashed. With them was a lady who had hurried over from her near-by farmhouse, undeterred by the explosions still erupting from the burning D-Dog. She asked them if they would like some tea, a kindly thought much appreciated by the crew who were devastated by the loss of Jim Crabtree. She hurried back to her home and soon returned with what must have been her best tea-set on a silver tray with a white lace cover.

Shortly afterwards an ambulance arrived with a RAF rescue crew who took them to Woodbridge where the MO quickly found contusions on various parts of Thorne, Harry Parker and Joe Keary. They were taken by ambulance to Ipswich Hospital

'for observation' while the other six were taken to the squadron where they learned that 10 aircraft had been lost on the Gelsenkirchen operation. Harry and Joe were passed OK after three days and returned to Downham Market. Thorne was kept for further treatment to a head injury but after a couple of days he also returned to the squadron, to find that the others had all gone on seven days leave. That left him with four days if the crew were to re-assemble at the same time, so with 'Tubby' Baker's blessing he left early the following day, breaking his journey home to call upon Jim Crabtree's parents.

On 25 October the crew resumed operations with a daylight raid on Essen.

CONFIDENTIAL.   RECOMMENDATION FOR IMMEDIATE AWARD.

RECOMMENDATION FOR HONOURS AND AWARDS.

Christian Names:- GEORGE ALEXANDER.   Surname:- THORNE.

Rank:-   PILOT OFFICER. (A/F/O).   Official No:- 174525.

Command & Group:- BOMBER. 8 (P.F.F.)   Unit:- No. 635 squadron, R.A.F.

Total hours flown on operations:-   79.45.   Since last award:- N/A.

Total number of sorties carried out:-   18.   Since last award:- N/A.

Appointment held:-   PILOT.   Recognition for which recommended:-   IMMEDIATE D.F.C.

Particulars of meritorious service:-

This officer was captain of an aircraft detailed to attack a heavily defended German target in daylight on 6th October, 1944.

On approaching the enemy coast, trouble developed in the port inner engine, with the result that further height could not be gained, and the aircraft was subjected to heavy and accurate fire from the German ground defences. Although the aircraft was hit many times, this officer, by expert captaincy and complete disregard of the opposition, pressed home his attack with the utmost determination and dropped his bombs accurately and on time. When leaving the target, the aircraft was again hit in the port side, damaging the fuel tanks and causing petrol leaks, which resulted in fire; eventually the fire was put out, but the aircraft being considerably lower than others engaged in the operation, was again subjected to heavy and light anti-aircraft fire.

By expert pilotage and cool judgment, F/O. Thorne avoided further damage to his aircraft, but on reaching enemy coast, the aircraft was again hit by heavy flak, resulting in the failure of the port outer engine, and the starboard rudder was also shot away. By skilful handling, under most difficult circumstances, the pilot brought his aircraft back to this country on the two remaining engines and decided to carry out a landing on an emergency airfield. As he was turning towards this airfield, the starboard inner engine failed, leaving only the starboard outer engine serviceable. Height was lost rapidly and F/O. Thorne, realising that he could not reach the airfield safely, made a crash landing in the first available field.

Throughout this action, this officer displayed exceptional qualities of leadership and coolness, and his determination and captaincy is deserving of the highest praise.

Date:- 21.10.44.

Wing Commander, Commanding,
No. 635 squadron, R.A.F.

REMARKS BY STATION COMMANDER.

Recommended for the immediate award of the Distinguished Flying Cross.

Date:- 21.10.44

Group Captain, Commanding,
R.A.F. Station, Downham Market.

COVERING REMARKS BY THE AIR OFFICER COMMANDING, PATH FINDER FORCE (NO. 8 GROUP).

Recommended.

Date:- 23rd October 1944.

Air Vice-Marshal, Commanding,
Path Finder Force (No. 8 Group).

4

'What a Way to Spend Boxing Day!'

So far as the weather was concerned, Christmas 1944 could be described as seasonal. Aircrews had another word for it, as did the British and American ground forces on the Continent struggling to maintain the Allied offensive in atrocious weather conditions. They had been more or less snowbound for weeks and most of our forward air bases in Europe were inoperative. There had been no let-up for Bomber Command however, in spite of repeated warnings from the Met experts of severe icing conditions with plenty of cumulo-nimbus cloud and associated electrical storms, with fog expected in many areas. Early in the evening on Christmas Day, battle orders were being posted up on notice boards in the Officers' and Sergeants' Messes at Downham Market. Six No 635 Squadron crews, including the Thorne crew, were detailed for briefing at 08.30hrs on the following morning, and the Squadron Commander, Wg Cdr 'Tubby' Baker, had his name on the list as captain of one of the other Lancasters.

It had been a miserable day weatherwise, with the threatened fog showing signs of materialising. Sure enough, within an hour of the briefing announcement it came down so quickly and so thickly that it seemed obvious the next day's operation would never get off the ground. Early calls were arranged to awaken the aircrew at 06.00hrs and after a light evening meal — the catering staff had excelled themselves with the mid-day Christmas dinner they had conjured up — everyone on the battle order set off through the blackness towards his billet with the intention of putting in as many sleeping hours as possible. At the same time they had little doubt that they would be awakened with the news that the op had been cancelled. When they did open their eyes at the call of 'wakey-wakey' however, the only information that the waker could give them was: 'It's foggy, and breakfast will be at a quarter to seven.'

Rose was the first to get his feet out of bed and go to the door of the billet. He took a quick look outside then quickly turned and said quietly 'Yes, it's foggy. You can't see a damn thing and its bloody cold.' Then, with tongue in cheek, he suggested a reason for the delay in cancelling what everyone believed would

be an impossible task: 'Someone at Bomber Command has had the idea that the mere suggestion of an op in these conditions will bring a quick return to reality after what he reckons has been too peaceful a Christmas for us!' More seriously, Rose and the others in the crew feared they might be close to the truth if they guessed that things were not going too well for the Allied forces fighting their way through the snow 'over there', and that urgent action by Bomber Command had been called for. It turned out that they were more than just close to the truth.

After the loss of Jim Crabtree on the ill-fated op to Gelsenkirchen in October, his place as wireless operator in the crew had been taken by Flt Lt Don Suttie whose crew had completed their required number of operations. He had joined them after their 13th trip, leaving that number of ops for him to do with another crew in order to complete his quota. All had gone well with the Thorne crew following their return to action after Gelsenkirchen, with Suttie establishing himself immediately as a quiet but genial character and an expert operator. His first trip with them was in a new Lancaster D-Dog for a daylight attack on the railway yards at Essen. His 12th trip was to Düsseldorf on Christmas Eve 1944. Only one more and he would have completed his tour. It was a particularly nerve-wracking time for all aircrews in that situation. What would be the last target? How long before we know? All this just to get the chop at the end? They were the kind of thoughts that constantly recurred in the minds of most of those who had so nearly done it all.

They did not appear to be worrying Suttie however, when he entered the Briefing Room with the other members of the Thorne crew after they had been served in the Mess with the inevitable pre-op meal of bacon and egg, rather blasphemously referred to in earlier days by members of the famous No 106 Squadron as 'the last supper'. Seated at their long trestle tables facing the platform, at the back of which was the black curtain covering a giant map of Europe, the members of the six crews waited for the CO to arrive. Few doubted he would announce that the operation was cancelled or that the take-off time had been put back

in the hope that the fog would lift. He arrived at 08.30hrs on the dot, followed as usual by his team of section officers.

When they had all taken their seats the CO, Wg Cdr 'Tubby' Baker, a veteran of 100 operations, went straight to the side of the black curtain, pulled the cord to reveal the illuminated map, uttered a laconic 'Well, there your are!' and then sat down on the edge of the table facing his audience. They knew where they were at that moment, but where they were supposed to be in six hours from then still remained of academic interest, so sure were they that a take-off would be impossible. The red tapes on the map marking the route indicated a target in an area unfamiliar to most of them. It was to be the cross-roads at St Vith, a small town in the thickly wooded Ardennes country in eastern Belgium.

'I know you are all expecting a scrub', said the CO, 'but until we get one it's business as usual. Nos 1, 3 and 5 Main Force Groups are laying on a total of 135 Lancasters, plus 63 Halifaxes from No 6 Group. In addition to the six from here, there will be five other Lancasters from PFF. I will be the Master Bomber. Our take-offs are supposed to start at 11.15hrs [the aircrew noted he said 'supposed to start' and not 'will start'] with times on targets from 13.28hrs to 13.42hrs. Twelve PFF Oboe Mosquitoes will be there to drop marker bombs from 15.23hrs to 15.35hrs.'

Since December 1942 the Pathfinders had built up a substantial Oboe Mosquito force in addition to its Lancasters, and they were an important tactical and strategical arm of the Group. With Oboe, bombs could be dropped within about 30ft of the target, and although the average range was restricted to approximately 350 miles, it took in vital targets such as the Ruhr — and St Vith. Unarmed, made almost entirely of wood and with twin Rolls-Royce Merlin engines, the Mosquito had a ceiling of 33,000ft and a maximum speed of 360mph. In addition to its target-marking role it was conspicuously successful in staging diversionary raids to attract enemy fighters away from the main bomber force.

After 'Tubby' Baker's short introduction to the briefing, the squadron Intelligence Officer took the floor. With the capture of

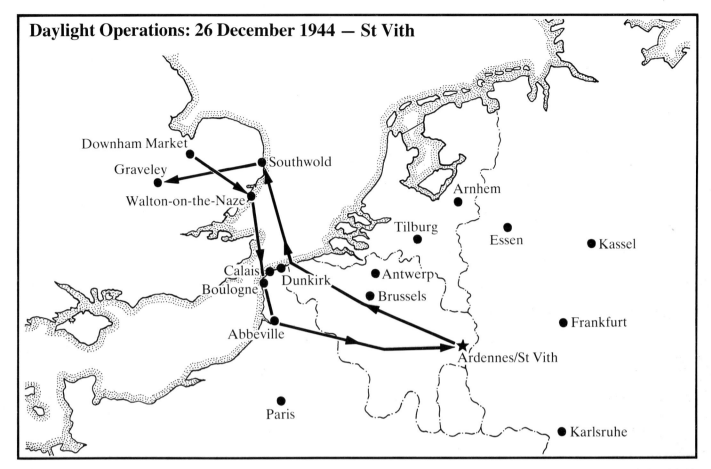

Daylight Operations: 26 December 1944 — St Vith

Paris, the Allied armies had crossed the Seine and pressed on in a northeasterly direction. The British Army on the left flank had captured Brussels and Antwerp, but the offensive came to a stop when they had to withdraw from Arnhem at the end of September 1944. There was a stalemate as the winter approached, and what a winter it was. Snow and fog descended upon the armies of both sides, and in many areas supplies could not get through. The weeks of misery stretched into months. Then came a dramatic change, not in the weather but in the activities of the German land forces.

On 16 December 1944 Don Bennett received a telephone call from the Senior Radar Controller at one of the PFF units which had been established on the Continent following the Allied breakthrough. His unit was based on one of the hills in the western part of the Ardennes, and he was telephoning to tell Bennett that he had been forced to retire from his base because the Germans had suddenly launched an attack through the Ardennes to the west, with the apparent intention of recapturing

Liège and Brussels and our supply port at Antwerp. Bennett immediately passed on the information to the Senior Allied Commanders but no-one appeared to take the threat very seriously. After all, the Germans, like the Allies, had been more or less snowbound for many weeks and there were no indications that the situation had improved, or would do so in the near future. They were soon to find out how wrong they had been. Montgomery was the only British commander to take the threat seriously, and he lost no time in bringing some of his troops down from the north to hold the spearhead 'of the German offensive which was under the command of Field Marshal von Runstedt.

The roads converged at St Vith from all directions and it was impossible to go from east to west without going through them. It was therefore of vital importance for supplies to the German spearhead. That was all understood and agreed by the listening crews, but how would they all get there in the present weather conditions? They waited for some clue from the Met Officer who was the next to address them. He came straight to the point: 'There is no sign of an early clearance', he said. 'The fog is widespread over England with the odd thinner patches here and there, and you will go into the clear at around 2,000-3,000ft. Over the Continent there is patchy fog but no cloud. Naturally we will know as soon as there is any change.'

In reply to the question 'Do you expect any early change?' he replied 'Frankly, no'. The remainder of the briefing followed the usual pattern. The Navigation Officer confirmed the route to and from the target

as shown on the map: over the Straits of Dover to the Somme, then eastwards to the Franco-Belgian frontier then northeast to St Vith, just north of the Luxembourg territory. He described the return route in terms of map references: 5017N 0610E 5050N 0520E to Southwold and on to base. At that point a WAAF entered the briefing room and handed a piece of paper to the CO. He quickly read what was on it and passed it to the Met Officer who immediately left the room. There were whispers of 'It's a scrub' from among the aircrew which were silenced when 'Tubby' Baker turned to the Nav Officer and said 'Sorry for the interruption, will you continue, please'. There was not much more for him to add however, because to save time he had held a separate meeting with his navigators immediately prior to the main briefing. The Signals Officer was the next to take the stage. His advice and instructions were familiar to all the W/Ops, but he asked them to see him after briefing, when he would give them details of the frequencies to be worked on this trip.

The Met Officer returned to the Briefing Room just before the Signals Officer sat down and after a short whispered conversation with the CO he held up the piece of paper brought in previously by the WAAF. With a gesture reminiscent of Chamberlain on his return from Berchtesgaden he announced: 'The fog shows some signs of clearing north of The Wash. All take-off times have been put back one hour. We'll let you know if there is any change.'

Without commenting on the Met news, 'Tubby' Baker resumed the briefing by calling upon the Bombing Leader. 'There seems to be a good chance that you will be able to see the target when you get there', he said. 'The Oboe Mossies will have marked the target ahead of the Master Bomber and his Deputy who are being supplied for this trip by another PFF squadron. You all know the drill and the bomb loads you will carry.'

If Lancaster D-Dog had been able to talk he would not have argued with the last part of that statement. He had been standing patiently at dispersal with a 10,000lb bomb and four 250lb target indicators in his belly since the early hours of the morning. As only six crews were concerned, all of them experienced in their jobs, the Bombing Leader did not prolong his briefing and when there was no reply to his 'any questions?' he concluded: 'The Master Bomber will give his instructions according to the circumstances of the moment and we can just hope that the visibility over the target will be better than it is here.' The Engineer Officer then took over, asked for questions, and there was none. The Flying Control Officer took his turn on the stage and begged for extreme caution in taxying to the take-off point at the eastern end of the east-west runway. He said groundcrews would be on hand to guide them from dispersal points 'if the fog continues'. He finished with: 'FIDO will be operating if necessary on landing. Call Control on your R/T as you cross the coast. Then follow our instructions.'

It would be appropriate here to interrupt the description of the briefing with the story of FIDO (Fog Investigation Dispersal Operation). The enemy's fighters and flak were obviously foremost among the dangers accepted by pilots and aircrews during the war. But natural hazards brought about by weather conditions were also the cause of many casualties. Fog conditions were the most feared and there were many occasions when aircraft had taken off in reasonable conditions, returning some hours later for the crews to find a complete clamp existing over a wide area of the country. Passed on by Ground Control from airfield to airfield in their efforts to find a possible landing place, they felt trapped in an impenetrable claustrophobic blackness. All they could do was press on and pray that their petrol would hold out. Too often it all ended in disaster in spite of the efforts of ground controllers, lacking the scientific and technical resources available to them today, to guide them to safety. And it was every pilot's nagging thought that one day or night it could happen to him. The advent of FIDO brought relief, the manner of which can best be described in the words of Don Bennett.

'I think it was about Christmas Eve 1943 that a moustached wing commander called Wooldridge* knocked at the front door of

---

* Wg Cdr John Wooldridge was Aeronautical Adviser to the Petroleum Warfare Department.

my quarters at Wyton and asked to see me. It was just about dinner time so I invited him in. He came diffidently inside the door and said he had some friends outside. Before inviting the friends in however, he waved a letter in my face and asked me to read it. I glanced at it and saw the signature was that of Winston Churchill. Briefly it said that the scientists had promised that fog could be cleared and that he wished all of those concerned to grant the best possible co-operation in bringing this about. I more than welcomed Wooldridge and asked him to bring in his companions. These proved to be Geoffrey Lloyd who was Minister of Petroleum Warfare, together with two of his advisers, Col Medlicott and Mr Hartley whom I had met in one of the petroleum companies in the Middle East. Needless to say, the idea of clearing fog was something which I more than welcomed. In fact I was simply staggered at the idea of the possibilities of such a device and I said so in no uncertain terms. The four visitors looked at each other and almost burst into laughter. They explained that the contrast of finding somebody who was keen to have fog cleared, compared to the discouragement and disappointment which had faced them for the entire previous 10hr in the northern groups was almost too much for them. The C-in-C Bomber Command was enthusiastic about the idea and sent them to the Main Force groups first as he did not wish me to be diverted by a development not peculiar to our needs.

'They stayed for dinner and during the meal we discussed the possibilities. I listened to their proposals and hopes, and to the requirements they laid down for the airfield on which an experiment could take place. They had been unable to find any airfield from the northern groups, all of whom made various excuses as to why it could not be arranged. I immediately nominated our airfield at Graveley as the most suitable and they enquired when they could inspect it. I replied 'immediately'. We got into a car and drove over to Graveley and they inspected it. I gave those people full credit for the magnificent way they then went about the installation of the equipment. They had 1,000yd of approach, and 1,000yd of runway equipped with FIDO burners within six weeks of my giving the OK to go ahead. The burners consisted of long lengths of pipe with the feed along a pipe over the burners so that the flame from each jet impinged slightly on this top feed tube, thereby vaporising the petrol that it fed along it and ensuring that no neat petrol came out of the jets but only pure vapour. It was not until the pure vapour came out that the smokiness of the flame disappeared and clean burning was

achieved. This was obviously essential if it were to improve visibility and not do the opposite. These burner pipes were laid parallel with the runway and about 50yd from it, thus the burners were a total of 150yd apart. They extended along each side of the runway and out into the approach area so that the intense heat which they generated cut a chasm through the fog which could be seen from above, and the aircraft could fly down into this chasm and land on the runway.

'The element of doubt was not only whether sufficient heat could be generated to disperse the fog as planned, but whether in view of the intense heat and glare of the flames it would be practical for an aircraft to land down the centreline of this inferno. To test this out I took a Lancaster from RAF Oakington over to Graveley one night and did the first landing with FIDO burning. I had vague thoughts of seeing lions jump through a hoop of flame at the circus. The glare was certainly considerable and there was some turbulence, but it was nothing to worry about and I expressed the view that FIDO was a usable project and should be developed at the utmost speed. I am pleased to say that we got it extended at Graveley and later on had it installed at Downham Market. Thus I was equipped with two airfields at which we could land with reasonable safety in practically all weathers.'

FIDO was to play an unusual part in the St Vith operation, but all 'Tubby' Baker said when he concluded the briefing which had taken less than one hour was 'It doesn't seem likely that many German fighters will be able to get off the ground'. And he smiled, shrugged his shoulders and half raised his arms in answer to a concerted 'Will we?' from the body of the hall. He continued: 'There won't be much heavy flak over the target but just to the west at Vielsam and near to Bastogne there will be a good deal of flak. Now check your watches. It's coming up to 4 minutes to 10.00hrs in 10 seconds — 5 seconds — 4 — 3 – 2 – 1 – NOW! 09.56. Good luck. See you later.'

The postponement announced at the briefing only strengthened the conviction, at least among the aircrew, that sooner or later the operation would be cancelled. When they pushed open the outside doors of the building to be faced with the now familiar blanket of fog, they were even more convinced that the scrub announcement could not be long in coming, and the sooner the better. But as 'Tubby' Baker

had said, until that message came from Group Headquarters it was business as usual. The immediate business therefore was to get themselves to the crew rooms about a couple of hundred yards away. They lay back slightly from the edge of the perimeter track, as did the briefing room, and knowing every feature of that part of the airfield they had no difficulty in locating it even though they could not see each other at more that five or six yards away. The crew rooms were in a single-storey concrete building which also housed the parachute store and the packing rooms. Flying clothing was kept in heated lockers. The parachutes, each one a personal issue, were in a permanently heated room. Every day the NCO in charge picked a number of 'chutes at random, and in the presence of the WAAFs responsible for them, the rip-cords were deliberately pulled. Aircrew were always welcome in the 'chute packing room and were encouraged to make visits and watch the girls doing their intricate work. Everyone had the utmost trust in them and Thorne never heard of a parachute failing its test either at the spot checks or the regular period checks, although a squadron leader air-gunner at Cranwell told him of an occasion which could have ended in disaster. He had come to Cranwell on a pilot's course after a long period operating in Defiant nightfighters earlier in the war. His parachute was due

Below:
Flt Sgt R. Martin RAAF (far left) watches his crew test their oxygen masks. *Pictorial Press*

for its regular period check after his return from a sortie during a Luftwaffe raid on Portsmouth. He threw his parachute into the boot of his car and went straight to bed intending to take it to the store in the morning. He forgot to do that, and in fact continued to use it for a further week. Then came a telephone call admonishing him for not returning his 'chute, and an order to bring it in immediately. There was no arguing with the WAAF on the other end of the line so he did as he was told. No time was lost when he arrived at the parachute room. The parachute was taken from him as he entered, the WAAF pulled the cord, and out dropped a useless soggy mass of white material. Without a word she pushed it to one side, gave him another 'chute and shook her head in a reproving manner as he made his apologies. That night, six out of the eight Defiants on his squadron were shot down. He was one of them, but he was lucky. He landed safely in a Kent hop field — by parachute.

It was 09.00hrs when the Thorne crew gathered together in the locker room and began to sort out their clothing for the trip. The heating installation in a Lancaster, as already explained, was adequate to the extent that the pilot, engineer, navigators and wireless op usually donned little more over their battle-dress, in addition to a parachute harness and Mae West jacket, than perhaps a woollen pullover in the winter. But on rare occasions the heating system had been known to fail so they always took with them Sidcot suits, flying boots and several pairs of gloves. That did not apply however to the two gunners. Jock Scott in the mid-upper turret benefited only slightly from the heating, and Jim Raymont isolated in his rear turret did not benefit at all. The gunners took their dressing procedures very seriously. Slowly and carefully were the important points, because any haste now with so much clothing caused perspiration. Even in winter, with air temperatures often registering minus 50°, patches of dampness developed. They would have been merely uncomfortable on the ground but in very low temperatures a damp patch almost inevitably resulted in frost-bite. The first item to be put on was an electrically heated suit, an all-in-one garment with wrist-length sleeves, thin slippers and a heating element woven throughout. Then three pairs of gloves — silk, electrically heated, and leather gauntlets. Two more pairs, suede and woollen, were also provided but rarely used. Then came a thick woollen jersey which reached down to the thighs and a pair of thick thigh-length woollen stockings. A Sidcot outer suit followed and finally black leather and suede flying boots. All that was left were Jim's parachute harness and Mae West which he would put on just prior to entering D-Dog.

With the take-off being put back one hour, there was plenty of time before making a move to dispersals. But the fog was still as thick as ever, especially over the open airfield, and by the time the call 'Transport up!' came from the outside door everyone remained mystified and, in the vernacular, cheesed-off with the events of the morning. Or as one cynic described them with his mind on a scrub, 'the non-events'. Two-and-a-half hours remained before the first aircraft was scheduled to take-off as they climbed aboard one of the three buses ready and waiting to convey them to D-Dog. 'Bus' seemed a rather grand official title bestowed upon an open vehicle with a canvas top, so they were always referred to as 'the wagons'. At a pinch, each wagon could just about cram in three crews with the paraphernalia for their flight. It was always augmented at the last minute by someone remembering to collect the ration boxes and bundle them into the arms of two or three of the passengers among the crews who sat facing each other on benches along each side of the wagon. The boxes, one for each crew, contained chocolate, barley sugar, chewing gum, raisins and flasks of coffee. There were times when things had gone well on a trip when the enjoyment of those simple items of refreshment caused some member of the crew to smack his lips and comment 'Jeese, that was worth coming for'. There were other times when circumstances had been such that the boxes were entirely forgotten during the trip and were handed back unopened on return to base.

With a cry from the back of 'All aboard!', the WAAF driver slipped into first gear and began to grope a way through the still thick-as-ever fog. There was another WAAF driver with her in the front to provide an extra pair of eyes on the journey around the perimeter track. It normally took two minutes to the dropping of the first of the crews at their aircraft's dispersal point. On this occasion it took 20min, with the driver never moving out of bottom gear. To cries of 'have a good trip', from inside and outside the wagon it was back into first gear and off to find the Thorne crew's aircraft. Being only two dispersals away, it was not expected to be too difficult, but driving in thick fog plays tricks with one's judgement of distance and time. When there were shouts of 'we must have passed it' from the passengers at the

Above left:
Flt Lt Ron Durran and his No 576 Squadron crew pictured in 1945, fully booted.

Left:
No 35 Squadron PFF crew. Standing, left to right: Flg Off Peters; Flt Lt Sculk; Wg Cdr Nicholls DFC; Flt Lt Jenkins; Flg Off Jones DFM; kneeling Plt Off Monk and Flg Off Sparks. The latter was the wireless operator whose real name could hardly have been more appropriate! *Flg Off Jones DFM*

back, the driver stopped and at that moment a couple of bobbing lights came towards them from the side.

There was a questioning shout of 'D-Dog?' from the direction of the lights followed by a cheer from the back of the wagon when the callers became visible and could be recognised as two stalwarts from the groundcrew. They had not been sitting in the warmth of their hut waiting for their aircrew to materialise out of the fog, but had decided to patrol the perimeter track in the vicinity of the dispersal point with the hope that they would be able to guide them towards the hard-standing where D-Dog stood impassively waiting for action. The performance at the wagon's first stop was repeated as the crew jumped out with their parachute packs and other paraphernalia as they wished the remaining crew in the wagon, and the WAAF drivers, a good trip. Guided by the groundcrew they went to the ladder near the rear of D-Dog's fuselage on the starboard side. One of the crew went up first to open the door which had been kept closed to keep out the fog as much as possible. Thorne followed with the other crew members hard behind him. There were still 1¾hr before take-off and although everyone was convinced there would be a scrub they would have to carry out as many of the pre-take-off checks as would be possible in the prevailing conditions. For instance, because he would be unable to see the harmonising boards through the fog, Jim had been unable to

check that his Browning guns were correctly adjusted. But he could be reassured in the knowledge that the squadron armourers had carried out the drill after D-Dog had returned from an operation two days previously to Düsseldorf.

When all the checks had been completed and without any snags being encountered, there was still more than one hour remaining before take-off, and the uncertainty of the whole business was beginning to generate an atmosphere almost of resentment. 'Why the hell can't they tell us what's happening?' was the general feeling among the crew. They stood kicking their heels outside the groundcrew's hut, too unsettled to stay inside in the warmth, when they heard the scuffling of feet coming towards them through the fog from the direction of the perimeter track. Simultaneously a reddish-yellow glow appeared from the same quarter and spreading in an east-west direction. 'Don't tell me', shouted Harry, 'they've activated FIDO. Some poor so-and-so is up there trying to get down'. No sooner had he spoken than 'Tubby' Baker materialised out of the fog followed by his car driven by a WAAF. He was wearing flying boots which accounted for the characteristic scuffling noise which preceded his appearance. The crew will never forget his words in what was a short and hurried conversation with Thorne:
'Do you think you can take off on FIDO, Alex?'

Above:
C-Charlie of No 101 Squadron crash-landed at Ludford Magna, alongside the FIDO pipelines

Right:
BEFORE AND AFTER. Flg Off T. N. Scholefield RAAF and his No 467 Squadron RAAF crew board Lancaster R5868, PO-S at Waddington on 11 May 1944 to attack Bourg-Leopold; while the second photograph shows the same crew being debriefed next morning. Attacked seven times by Junkers Ju88 night fighters, they failed to locate the target, jettisoned the 12,000lb bomb load into the North Sea and returned. Long described as R5868's 100th operational sortie, in fact this was its 91st op.

'Gawd knows, I've never tried.'

'Well here's our chance. The fog is clearing from the north, just about enough for Main Force for take-off, so somehow we have got to get airborne. You will be number two for take-off after me, at 13.17hrs. I'll go and find the others now. Best of luck, see you later.'

With that he went to the front of his car which had been manoeuvred to a few feet away, waved his arms for the driver to follow him back to the perimeter track and disappeared into the murk to carry the glad tidings to the five other crews.

Between the flames

FIDO was essentially a landing aid, and without being too dramatic it would be a case of venturing into the unknown to attempt a take-off on it. When the final approach to a landing was being made the pilot could see the two lines of fire stretching below and ahead so he simply followed the normal procedures and landed between them. The aircraft did tend to hold off and float more than in a normal landing due to the heat produced by the lines of burning petrol but, once the wheels touched down, control of the aircraft was no more difficult than in normal visibility. The unknown factors in the present situation were the take-off with the extra weights of over 11,000lb bomb load and 2,000gal of petrol. And how would the heat and glare from the FIDO installation affect the take-off with the aircraft gathering speed, as opposed to reducing it to a standstill on a landing? No one could say, so Thorne and Harry agreed they would take it as it came and act accordingly — or words to that effect. And if Thorne had known how that phrase would be repeated *ad nauseam* in later years by the gods of football on television, he would have used different words to that effect!

The main problem, as it appeared to him, might be the possibility of FIDO becoming a massed red glare reflected in the fog to the front as well as on both sides as the aircraft speed increased from a standstill up to and beyond the lift-off at around 110mph. In that case he would have to depend on his reading of the instruments in order to keep a straight course until the glare became lost behind them. But then, he thought, why should that be difficult? After all, he would be climbing entirely on instruments until they were in the clear at 3,000ft or so, if the Met boys were correct in their forecast. One thing he had decided with the crew was that they should allow plenty of time for the half-a-mile or so journey around the perimeter track in the fog to the end of the east-west runway for take-off. There was time for a chat with the groundcrew who told them that some of their colleagues — they did not know how many — from the aircraft not flying, would be on each side of the perimeter track with torches to help guide them to the take-off point. Then, after the last cigarette for at least the next five hours, Thorne led the way to the bottom of the ladder into D-Dog. The time was 12.50hrs when everyone was in position and settled down with intercoms switched on for him to make the individual crew checks starting at the back: 'Okay Jim?' 'Okay Skipper'. 'Okay Jock?' 'Okay Skipper' . . . and so on until he said 'Right, so am I. We'll get cracking.' Sliding his window back, he put his head out and shouted 'All ready down there?' to the airman standing below with the trolley accumulator plugged into the port inner engine. In a few seconds the propeller turned slowly and gathered speed until the fog was swirling backwards above and

below the wing. The revs were then reduced, and when the other three engines had received similar treatment to Thorne's and Harry's satisfaction it was 'Chocks away!' and the slow trundle through the fog commenced. (A thorough check of the engines had, of course, been carried out during the main checks on the aircraft an hour previously.)

Sure enough, there was an airman with a torch-light just visible on the port side. There was no difficulty in making the short distance from the aircraft's hard standing to the perimeter track where they turned left and were picked up by a succession of airmen on the port side. It was slow going but it worked well, and Thorne turned D-Dog round on to the approach to the standpoint at a right angle to the runway, which was somewhere in the middle of the reflected glare from FIDO, now appearing as a vast orange-red curtain of fog towering in front on the starboard side. He moved tentatively forward until a red light was waved and he could just discern the blurred outline of the rear fuselage of another Lanc at a stand-still in front. 'That must be "Tubby" ', said Reg Keary who had been keeping a look-out from the bomb aimer's compartment in the nose of D-Dog. 'And we've got another just behind us', came Jim Raymont's voice over the intercom. 'Good', replied Thorne. 'Let's hope the other three have made it. Keep listening and I'll tell you when "Tubby" moves so that you'll be ready for the off.' It was a fidgety eye-straining wait until Reg called 'He's moving'. A split second later the sound of Tubby's engines revving up indicated that the CO was turning right on to the runway unseen by those in the fog behind him who would follow. There was silence for perhaps two minutes, and at exactly 13.17hrs came the — at first — gentle roar of the four Merlin engines increasing to a straining crescendo as the Baker crew headed between the flaming burners towards lift-off. Then everything seemed to happen in rapid succession. A torch-light, green this time, was waved in a forward motion in front of D-Dog followed by another torch, white now, swinging to the right. Almost immediately came another red and Thorne brought D-Dog to a stop. Now he could distinguish the flames from the burners stretching ahead at the bottom of the glare on each side and he waited for the final green. With the speed increasing as the throttles were advanced, Thorne found that the flames maintained their identity within the glare and there was no more difficulty in keeping a straight course than on a normal take-off. The tricky bit came when the burner flames were suddenly left behind, and immediate attention had to be concentrated on the compass and air-speed indicators.

At 120mph Thorne and Harry went through the routine of throttling back the engines to climbing power, wheels up and locked and flaps up, at the end of which Graham Rose came through with the course for the first turning point over The Naze on the coast six miles south of

Harwich. He would tell Thorne 30sec before the change of course should be made. The Naze was the rallying point for the Main Force aircraft from the north, and Thorne hoped that D-Dog would be above the fog before that point was reached. He did not relish the possibility of getting mixed up with any early birds out of the 289 other aircraft which would be converging on that spot, and all aircraft were restricted to a height of 2,000ft until the enemy coast was reached in order to keep below the height at which they could be picked up by the German radar. The change of course at The Naze was made at just under 2,000ft, a height which would be maintained until the second change when the French coast was reached at the mouth of the Somme river.

There had been no improvement in the fog condition, with the wing-tips only just visible. At 14.06hrs Boris confirmed his 'Gee' position when he identified the Somme and the town of Abbeville on his H2S screen. That was the next turning point in the direction of the Ardennes. It was also the point at which Harry started unloading his Window at the prescribed intervals. They were now climbing from the 2,000ft limit and the fog was losing its density, until at 3,000ft they were almost in the clear with fog patches below and a few banks of white cloud in front of them. Within a few minutes, whilst they were still climbing, Jim Raymont reported sightings of Lancs behind him at heights of 3-5,000ft above them and, as was to be expected, no signs of enemy fighters. Neither was there any opposition from ground defences apart from sporadic bursts of light flak well to port.

At 15.00hrs Gray gave Thorne a slight alteration in course to starboard. They were spot on time and should unload their target indicators and the bomb at 15.25hrs, as scheduled. Reg reported 'All ready' for the run-up to the target with the hope that there would be no interference from fog patches. The navigators remained happy about the timing; Don and the gunners were ready for anything that was to come; Harry, thankful to be rid of his Window, kept a roving eye on his instruments; and Thorne listened out for the voice of the Master Bomber who he knew would be watching out for the preliminary cascade of markers from the Oboe Mosquitoes.

Thorne wondered if the MB could see the Mossies, because he couldn't. Then, 20min later it all started. The first marker

Top right:
MASTER BOMBERS. Wg Cdr Maurice Smith DFC (far left) who (among other ops) was 'MC' of the notorious Dresden raid on 13 February 1945; while on the right is Wg Cdr John Woodroffe, generally acknowledged as the 'doyen' of Master Bombers. *Late Wg Cdr M. Smith DFC*

Right:
DEBRIEFING. A No 9 Squadron crew are interrogated. *Via W. R. Chorley*

from a still unseen Mosquito burst in a circle of yellow. It was followed in rapid succession by four more, all within a radius of 50yd. The Deputy MB's voice came immediately over the radio: 'Markers gone!' The MB would then be making his run-up to assess his Deputy's accuracy. His call came 'Bomb the reds!' On their heels came the Thorne crew, both at 8,000ft, then the other Pathfinders, and the procession of Main Force aircraft. Of the total of 295 aircraft, 279 dropped their bombs with only sporadic bursts of heavy flak from the guns of the ground defences. D-Dog made a rock-steady run with the guidance of Reg Keary, and the resulting photograph showed his aim had been spot on. Only two aircraft, both Halifaxes, failed to return; one of them was shot down on the last leg to the target and the other disappeared off Ramsgate. One other, hit in the rear turret, landed badly damaged in France. Presumably, the remaining 13 which did not reach the target did not get airborne, or had to return because of some malfunction.

Interpretation reports on photographs taken on 27 December the following day, showed craters honeycombing all roads through and out of the town, also craters in the railway sidings and damage to the railway bridge. Further photographs taken between 29 December and 11 January showed all road and rail communications impassable with the exception of two roads which appeared to have been repaired. Two raids by the US 8th Air Force on 29 December and 11 January contributed to the success of the overall operation to halt the German breakthrough after the PFF Oboe Controller in the Ardennes had made his warning phone call to Don Bennett on 16 December. The German forces with their tanks were soon left

without fuel and ammunition. For them it was the end of the Battle of the Bulge. For the Allies there was the prospect of an early end to what had been a bitter land battle against the enemy and the elements. Later, the air attacks on the Ardennes were described by Tedder as 'Beyond praise', and by Eisenhower as '. . . having achieved the impossible on behalf of the Army'.

The return flight from St Vith had been uneventful so far as the Thorne crew was concerned, apart from a return to the same fog conditions they had left behind. So FIDO would be operating again, but this time for landing. As the English coast was crossed at Southwold, Don Suttie transmitted a message to base advising them of the fact. None of them could believe their ears when Don relayed the reply he had received: 'Aircraft accommodation full. Divert to RAF Graveley.' There were cries over the intercom of 'I can't believe it!', 'We can't land at our own airfield now!', 'Who's going to sleep in my bed?' and others not fit for publication. While using up their stock of vituperation, Gray had been working out the course to Graveley which lay 40 miles southwest of Downham Market. They landed there on FIDO at 17.55hrs, and when Thorne went to report at Flying Control he found 'Tubby' Baker had just beaten him to it.

It turned out that Main Force airfields were suffering a return to fog conditions and their returning aircraft were being diverted to airfields as far away as Scotland and southwest England. For the same reason, the six No 635 Squadron aircraft were found resting places only a comparatively short distance from home. The fear of all the crews was that they might not be able to take-off for Downham Market the next day if the fog persisted.

Although the operation had not proved difficult, the day itself had been an unsettled and tiring one. After they had enjoyed a drink, a good meal and then another drink there was nothing the 635 types wanted more than a spot of bed. That did not prove too easy because there were crews from more than a dozen other diverted aircraft ready and waiting to get their heads down. It was close on midnight when Sqn Ldr 'Pop' Hemming, Flying Controller at Graveley and a veteran of World War 1, came into the Mess in his dressing gown and carpet slippers. Seeing the Thorne crew still there, he said: 'Haven't they found you beds yet? Come with me and we'll see what we can find.' Picking up all their belongings, they followed 'Pop' with his torch into the cold and foggy night. It was half-an-hour before he found a Nissen hut with no one in it, but with a dozen made-up beds. Cold and damp though it was, they thanked 'Pop' for his help, wished him a good trip back to the Mess, threw themselves dressed as they were on to the beds, and next thing they knew was being gently wakened by an airman and presented with a cup of tea. The time, he told them, was 7 o'clock. It was still dark outside but they found the Mess, revelled in the warmth for a few minutes, enjoyed the first wash in more than 24hr, and went in to breakfast. Their one desire was to get back to Downham Market but 'Pop' Hemming was still in bed and it took some time for them to persuade the Graveley Flying Control that they could make the short journey in spite of the fog which, in the light of day, could be seen to have cleared considerably overnight. Eventually they landed back 'home' at mid-day and then — the reason for their anxiety to get back to Downham — they started preparing to go on leave to commence the next day.

They returned on 4 January. The following three nights were spent going to, over and from Hanover, Hanau and Munich. Then the snow came to England and for the next four days the station's daily summary of events reported: 'No operations. Weather nine to ten-tenths cloud, at times as low as 400ft. All crews spent major part of the day clearing snow.'

It would be wrong to say that the last traces of snow had been cleared off the main runway and perimeter track when the last 'volunteer' threw his shovel into the collecting lorry in the late afternoon on 12 January 1945. There was still plenty of slush and ice around on 14 January when D-Dog took off at 19.45hrs on what was to be one of the most complex operations undertaken by Bomber Command. And that, as they say, is another story.

The next, in fact.

Left:
Another op completed – another day to live . . .

5
Striking Oil

There can be few more depressing sights than that presented by a snowbound airfield. Nothing creates an increasing mood of frustration among aircrew more than days' and nights' inaction such as those endured by the whole of Bomber Command in the early part of January 1945.

Every member of a Pathfinder crew had undertaken to aim at a minimum of 45 operations, and throughout No 635 Squadron there was a general feeling of relief and 'let's get on with it' when the weather showed signs of clearing on 13 January. Six crews in the squadron were detailed for a main briefing at 16.45hrs on the following day. The Thorne crew in Lancaster D-Dog were among the six named, but there was some doubt that Jim Raymont, who had been rear gunner on all their 34 operations to date, would be with them on the trip. He had not looked too well for a couple of days but he assured everyone when the briefing detail was announced that he 'would be okay tomorrow'. He was persuaded however to see the squadron's

doctor who found he had an incipient carbuncle on his neck and declared him unfit for flying. With only six crews being required from the squadron, there were plenty of gunners available so Sqn Ldr Frank Kelsh, the Gunnery Leader, proposed to Thorne that WO Ken Paige, an old hand at the job and nearing the end of his tour, should take Jim's place in the rear turret. There had been one other change in the crew. Following the departure of Don Suttie after the St Vith trip, his place as wireless operator was taken by Ernest Patterson who had completed 29 operations with another No 635 Squadron crew which had lost three of its members. Ernie remained with the Thorne crew until the end of the war.

Below and overleaf, top:
Snow might look pretty on Christmas cards but was not welcomed by operational crews. This scene is at Waddington on 1 March 1944 with Lancs of No 463 Squadron RAAF 'well-wintered'.

The crew on the Leipzig raid would therefore be: Alex Thorne (Pilot), Graham Rose (Navigator), Boris Bressloff (2nd Nav and Radar Operator), Ernest Patterson (Wireless Operator), Harry Parker (Flight Engineer), Reg Keary (Bomb Aimer), Jock Scott (Mid-Upper Gunner), Ken Paige (Rear Gunner). The late-lamented D-Dog that had battled so gallantly to reach safety on the return trip from Gelsenkirchen in October, only to succumb within sight of the emergency runway at Woodbridge, had been replaced by a new D-Dog which had all the attributes of its predecessor. The crew would be acting as Visual Centrers on the target, together with Flt Lt Mellor's crew. The crews of Sqn Ldr Mange, Flg Off Beattie, Flg Off Melling and Flg Off Westhorpe would act as Blind Markers in the event of the target being obscured by cloud or fog.

Having settled the rear gunner business, Thorne left Frank Kelsh's office in the darkness of the winter evening on the 5min walk to his billet. From behind him came

Above:
Out on a frozen dispersal, armourers begin loading a 4,000lb HC/HE 'Cookie'.

the sound of a Lancaster's engines being revved up at its dispersal point on the other side of the airfield. It was good to hear it after the days of silence. As he walked past the ancient Bexwell village church there was a faint sound of organ music, probably the organist running through his hymns for the Sunday services. Two worlds, he thought, contrasting the peaceful sound with the stuttering roar from the Lanc. He quickened his steps to get to the billet before Gray and Boris left to go to the Mess for dinner. They were just putting on their uniform jackets as he pushed open the outside door, closed it behind him (remembering the blackout) and then on through the inner doorway into the brightness and warmth of their sleeping quarters. Here was their resting place, sometimes at night and at other times during the day, according to what was happening in the bigger world. They waited for him to wash and change, and within half-an-hour they were sharing in a round of drinks in the Mess with some of their colleagues from the other five crews who were on the next day's battle order. By 10 o'clock they were all in bed.

Thorne had arranged to meet the replacement rear gunner at D-Dog's dispersal at 9 o'clock on the following morning. When he arrived there Ken Paige had already started checking the four Browning guns in the rear turret. Thorne left him to it after arranging to meet him when he had finished the job, either in the groundcrew's hut or, if it should be nearby at the time, at the NAAFI wagon which toured the dispersal points during the morning dispensing tea and wads.

By mid-morning Ken and the other members of the crew had completed their pre-op checks and in response to calls of 'NAAFI up!' from the groundcrew, they all collected at the wagon which had stopped near D-Dog's dispersal area. Activity was building up around them as they downed their mugs of tea or coffee handed to them by NAAFI ladies over the let-down counter in the side of their wagon. Trolleys loaded with bombs were being pulled along the airfield perimeter track to deliver their cargoes to the six aircraft of No 635 Squadron involved in the night's operations. It required considerable skill on the part of the driver of a tractor pulling the bomb trolleys to manoeuvre into a position beneath an aircraft so that the bombs could be hoisted off the trailer and winched up into the bomb bay. Some of the drivers were WAAFs and their male colleagues were never lacking in praise for the skills they demonstrated in a job which was not without its dangers. (The late Air Cdre John Searby — he was the Master Bomber on the famous raid on the enemy's secret weapon establishment at Penemünde on 17/18 August 1943 — always said he would never forget the day at RAF Scampton when a trolley train loaded with 4,000lb bombs exploded, killing the

WAAF driver and destroying, one by one, 12 Lancasters.) The petrol bowsers were also in evidence and although they had not yet got around to D-Dog, Thorne had been told by the groundcrew that the aircraft were being tanked up with a full load. So it was to be a long trip, perhaps up to 8hr. There was nothing more for them to do at dispersal so they all mounted their bicycles and set off around the perimeter track to the squadron buildings where they split up to go to their respective section offices.

When Gray, Boris and Thorne came together again in the Mess at lunch time, they and the others on the battle order were unanimous in their guesses that the target that night would be in the Berlin, Leipzig or Nuremburg areas. Wherever it turned out to be it was unlikely they would be able to 'go to bed properly', as poor old Jim Crabtree used to say, for at least 15hr. The pre-op meal was to be served at 16.00hrs so after an early and light lunch they cycled back to their billet for, they hoped, a couple of hours' sleep before making their way to the briefing room. They knew they would feel awful when they did wake up and stagger out into the cold and already darkening evening, but at the end of the 5min walk which led into the light and warmth of the Mess, everyone was feeling better. The inevitable — but always enjoyed — operational bacon and

Left:
In the bomb dump, armourers prepare a load of incendiary canisters — despite the weather. *IWM CH14534*

egg, plus a sausage on this occasion, were quietly consumed and then it was everybody out again to the waiting transport to take them to the briefing room. There again there was warmth and light with the familiar layout of tables, and the giant map on the end wall which would soon be uncovered to reveal the target for the night.

By the time the briefing came to an end the elaborate pattern of the night's operations was as complex as any they had known. The attacks were planned in two time phases. Each contained an attack on the Leuna oil plants at Merseburg to the west of Leipzig, involving penetration through an area known as the Coblenz-Frankfurt gap, to a depth of 250 miles behind the battlefront established at that time by the advancing Allied forces. There were also to be two attacks on Berlin by Pathfinder Mosquitoes. A total of 1,215 aircraft would be engaged. The six Lancasters from No 635 Squadron would attack Merseburg/Leuna oil plants (Phase 2), as the battle order below shows:

TARGET	GROUP	AIRCRAFT	NUMBERS	TIME OVER TARGET
First Phase				
1. *Merseburg/Leuna*	5	*Lancaster*	210	*20.47-21.15*
	1	*Mosquito*	8	*20.47-21.15*
	1	*Lancaster*	8	*20.47-21.15*
2. *Grevenbroich*	6	*Halifax*	136	*19.33-19.43*
Marshalling	PFF	*Lancaster*	3	*19.32-19.40*
Yards	PFF	*Mosquito*	12	*19.30-19.32*
3. *Berlin*	PFF	*Mosquito*	41	*20.35-20.45*
4. *Mannheim*	PFF	*Mosquito*	9	*19.59-20.18*
5. *'Sweepstake'*	7	*Lancaster/Halifax*	60	
Division	91	*Wellington*	19	
	92	*Wellington*	24	
		Wellington	23	
Second Phase				
6. *Merseburg/Leuna*	1	*Lancaster*	245	*23.53-00.12*
	6	*Lancaster*	53	*23.52-00.08*
	PFF	*Lancaster*	57	*23.51-23.59*
	PFF	*Mosquito*	6	
7. *Dulmen*	4	*Halifax*	100	*23.13-23.35*
	PFF	*Lancaster*	3	*23.20*
	PFF	*Mosquito*	12	*23.12-23.17*
8. *Berlin*	PFF	*Mosquito*	42	*23.56-00.11*
9. *Minelaying*	1	*Lancaster*	10	*22.46-23.02*
	4	*Halifax*	10	*22.47-23.09*
	6	*Halifax*	11	*23.10-23.30*
10. *Bomber Support*	100	*Lancaster* *Halifax* *Liberator* }	107	
Signals Patrols	100	*Halifax*	5	
11. *Met Recce*		*Mosquito*	1	

As the briefing progressed the reasons behind the planning of the night's operations on such a wide scale became clear. In the 1930s scientists on both sides had been working on the development of new radio and radar techniques. The Germans had produced *Würzburg*, a mobile radar set which could plot unseen aircraft for their anti-aircraft defences to fire at with accuracy up to a range of 25 miles. They also had *Freya*, a mobile early warning system that could plot aircraft up to a range of 75 miles with a 360° cover, but it could not tell how high they were. The RAF did have Chain Home, an early warning system with a range of 120 miles made possible only with the aid of 300ft high aerials. It could measure an aircraft's altitude but only within an arc of 120°. The Germans were undoubtedly ahead in the early days of the war and the production of radar aids became a constant 'anything you can do, we can do better' battle between the two sides with their introductions of measures and countermeasures. Two of the latter featured prominently in the attacks on 14 January, as they did in many other Bomber Command operations during 1942 and after.

As far back as 1937 Dr R. V. Jones at the Air Ministry Directorate of Scientific Intelligence had started investigating the effects of metal strips dropped from aircraft to jam the enemy's radar plotting of approaching aircraft. The result was codenamed 'Window' — bundles of metal foil strips dropped from aircraft in the bomber stream at correctly timed intervals between set points en route to the target. The strips floated to earth causing havoc on the German fighter control radar screens and made accurate plotting of approaching aircraft virtually impossible. The second countermeasure was codenamed 'Mandrel'. Its object was to jam the German *Freya* system by having a small number of aircraft orbit individually in a line whilst they produced interference via microphones installed in an engine of each aircraft. They had a similar effect on the German fighter controllers' radar screens as does a car with an unscreened ignition on a domestic television screen. Eight aircraft in each phase orbiting that night in set positions were planned to produce an effective 'Mandrel' screen stretching from Brussels to Verdun to defeat the efforts of the enemy's fighter controllers.

At the briefing the Met officer had forecast clear conditions at take-off continuing over England apart from ground fog in places. There would be broken cloud at first over the Continent increasing to 10/10ths stratocumulus with ground fog and smoke as the target was approached. Icing conditions were probable over

Above:
John Searby — 'Honest John' to his colleagues — who was Master Bomber over Peenemunde on 17/18 August 1943. An ex-Halton aircraft apprentice, Searby rose through the ranks to retire eventually as Air Commodore, CBE, DSO, DFC. *IWM CH8485*

Below:
STILL LIFE. The last moments before leaving.

5,000ft from the start. Winds would be variable in strength and direction over the whole of the route. A front was building up from the north and it would probably reach No 100 and PFF Groups at around 02.00hrs. None of that was very encouraging for the crews.

Wg Cdr 'Tubby' Baker, in his sixth month as squadron CO, detailed the support which would be provided for the aircraft in the attacks on the main target, the Leuna oil plant. Phase 1 would open with the raid on Grevenbroich in the Ruhr area, whilst the aircraft in the 'Sweepstake' Force were flying over the North Sea and Heligoland to draw northern-based enemy fighters away from the bombers heading towards their mainland targets. It was clear that the tactics throughout the night were aimed to cause such confusion within the enemy's raid-tracking and fighter control organisations that they would be unable to cope with the number of attacks to be carried out within the two phases. Twice to Leipzig and Berlin, and once each to the Ruhr, Dortmund and Mannheim, plus the

diversionary operations and minelaying, made it quite a night for Bomber Command. The crews concerned could only hope that the strategy and the tactics to be employed would be successful.

It was a clear night with only patches of ground fog, as Met had forecast, when the Thorne crew took off at 19.50hrs with a load of six 1,000lb TIs and four 500lb bombs. Beacon lights were flashing below as the undercarriage and flaps were raised and within seconds the roofs of Downham Market could just be discerned, as quickly to disappear into an opaque nothingness and become a black inverted bowl devoid of movement and life. At around 750ft Thorne swung over to port and, still climbing, headed south for Beachy Head at which point all navigation lights would be switched off and courses would be set to cross the French coast at Dieppe. All aircraft were to keep below 8,000ft and there was to be radio silence until they emerged on the other side of the 'Mandrel' screen stretching in a line from Brussels down to Verdun, 50 miles west of the battle front. Jim Raymont and Jock in the gun turrets kept the rest of the crew informed on the increasing number of Main Force aircraft as they merged from their flights from the Nos 1 and 6 Group bases into a stream behind the leaders over Reading. From then on there were, according to the plan, 355 Lancasters and six Mosquitoes on their way to Leipzig. Also on the scene were 100 Halifaxes, three Lancasters and 12 Mosquitoes. That force would branch north 50 miles before reaching the 'Mandrel' screen and round the east of the Ruhr to Dulmen near Munster. Some 100 miles to the north 42 Mosquitoes were making a second high level attack on Berlin, 31 Lancasters and Halifaxes over the North Sea were minelaying and, somewhere, there were 10 support aircraft from No 100 Group. No one, to Thorne's knowledge, ever asked what the latter were to do, or afterwards, what they had done. Whatever it was, the Group which specialised in secret and unusual activities was sure to have made a good job of it.

At 20.18hrs Reg Keary, down in his bomb-aimer's compartment, came on the intercom: 'I think I can see the coast. Can you, Skip?' Thorne could not see it from his position and Boris interjected: 'He's not wrong you know. I've got a perfect fix on the coastline. I reckon we should be over Beachy Head in 5min.' Then, from Gray: 'There's only one snag. We're 2min ahead of schedule. Do you want to lose them now or later?' Thorne answered: 'We don't know what sort of reception we'll get on the other side, so I'll start losing it now. Keep your eyes open for other aircraft.' Ken Paige came on to say that the nav lights on the aircraft following were going

Left:
TAKE-OFF.

Night Operations: 14-15 January 1945 — Main Target Leipzig

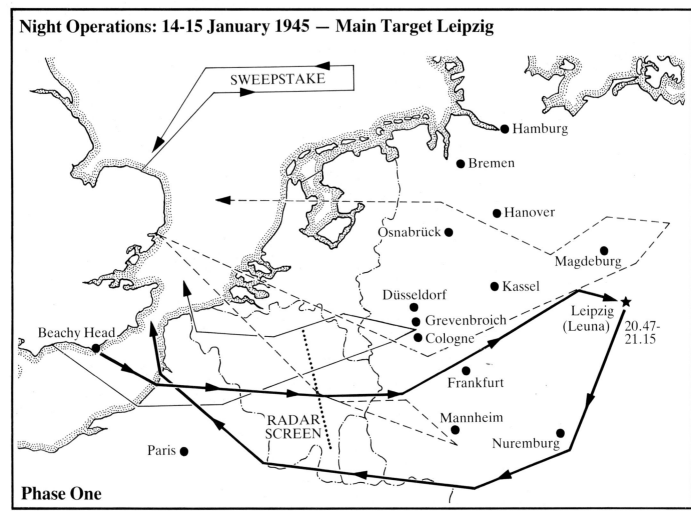

SWEEPSTAKE

Hamburg

Bremen

Hanover

Osnabrück

Magdeburg

Düsseldorf

Grevenbroich

Cologne

Kassel

Leipzig (Leuna) 20.47-21.15

Beachy Head

Frankfurt

Mannheim

RADAR SCREEN

Paris

Nuremburg

Phase One

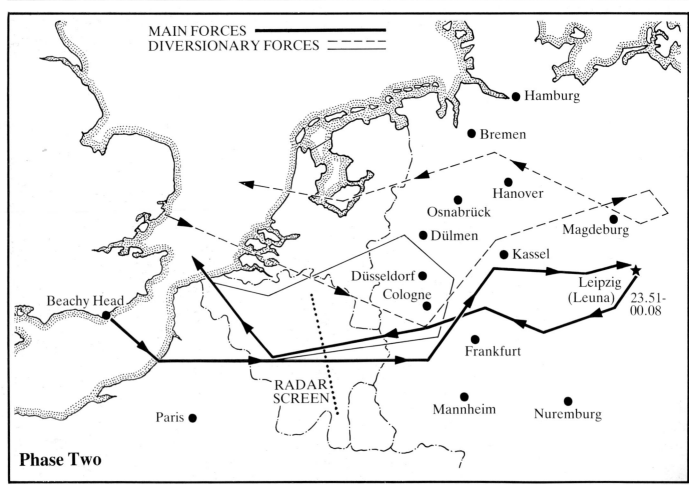

MAIN FORCES ——————
DIVERSIONARY FORCES – – – –

Hamburg

Bremen

Hanover

Osnabrück

Dülmen

Magdeburg

Düsseldorf

Cologne

Kassel

Leipzig (Leuna) 23.51-00.08

Beachy Head

Frankfurt

RADAR SCREEN

Paris

Mannheim

Nuremburg

Phase Two

out fairly rapidly. Thorne replied: 'We'll keep ours on for a bit. I'll lose some height to get below the others while we do a dog-leg. Starting now.' They crossed the coast as he was speaking.

Despite the darkness it was usually easy, in clear conditions of course, to tell where land ended and water began. It appeared several shades lighter than the land, not unlike comparing black with purple, and one could see an unmistakable contrast. Thorne could now just make out the outline of Eastbourne and as he turned to port 30° he reduced the revs slightly to lose height. After one minute he turned to starboard 60° and in another minute he rolled 30° to port back on to the original course, advancing the revs to regain height. Gray came over with a new course heading for Dieppe and was keeping his fingers crossed with a hope that they had lost the superfluous minutes, and that there would be no further drastic changes in wind speeds and direction such as those which had upset their timing to Beachy Head. Apart from that easily corrected situation everything was going smoothly. Harry had been occupied in his gauges: oil pressures and temperatures, coolant temperatures, fuel contents and pressures, and in writing up his log. Reg, Ken and Jock had been keeping a continuous look-out for any signs of enemy action and also possible danger of collisions with other aircraft in the stream. Even on the flight down to Beachy Head from base, when all the aircraft were showing their navigation lights, Thorne had received sudden warnings from one of the three of aircraft flying too close for comfort. To be fair, perhaps the crew of that aircraft were at the same time warning *their* pilot of the situation. The difference of a mere two degrees in their headings at speeds of 180-200mph at the same heights could bring them together in a matter of seconds. Rarely did any crew complete a night operation without their stomachs turning over when there occurred sudden crashing bumps as their aircraft hit the slipstreams of unseen aircraft veering across their path. One could be amazed at the comparatively few losses attributed to aerial collisions if it were not for the now recognised fact that it was impossible, for obvious reasons, to give anything like an accurate figure. The order for signals silence until crossing the 'Mandrel' screen resulted in Ernie Patterson concentrating on listening out for any messages that might come from Group such as a recall, but that was extremely unlikely. Meanwhile D-Dog continued to behave impeccably.

Once again Reg claimed the first sighting of land and Boris gave out the glad news that Dieppe would be reached on time at 21.04hrs. Gray gave Thorne the new course, 045°, and they flew on towards the Frankfurt area. To emphasise a break between Phase 1 and Phase 2 in an endeavour to discount the possibility of further attacks, the 'Mandrel' screen had ceased to radiate at 20.25hrs, recommencing at 21.30hrs. That tactic appeared to be successful because there were very few signs of opposition from the defences. The 'Mandrel' screen was so far proving effective and at 22.00hrs the Leipzig and Dulmen forces emerged through the screen on their easterly courses approximately 20 miles apart. They had separated 20min earlier, the Dulmen force to go north around the eastern side of the Ruhr to its target. The effect of the manoeuvre was to create a mass of confused plotting which prevented the enemy making any accurate track of the Dulmen raid being formed and disguising the raid on the Leuna oil installations until it was well into the Kassel area. When that track was eventually sorted out the Luftwaffe and ground defences were further confused by the appearance of the Mosquitoes on Berlin.

As the Main Force of 355 Lancasters was nearing Kassel it turned east. Only then could it have been apparent to the air and ground defences that Leuna was to be the target — for the second time that night. When the 'Mandrel' jamming on the first phase had died away the German fighters had returned to their bases. There must

Below:
Mid-air collisions were a constant hazard in main streams of bombers. Here Z-Zebra of No 207 Squadron displays its port wing-tip damage after colliding with a No 57 Squadron Lanc over Stuttgart on the night of 12/13 September 1944. *R. Winton*

have been complete confusion among the fighter control units and during the first phase there had been only slight interception by a few fighters north of Frankfurt. When it was apparent that a second phase was developing the controllers, in desperation, switched their fighter units covering Berlin to Leuna. But they were too late. Furthermore, the switch meant that those fighters were not around when 42 PFF Mosquitoes attacked the 'Big City' — again for the second time that night.

So everything had continued to go well for the forces of Bomber Command — except for one thing. From the point where the Dulmen force had parted company with the aircraft on the major Leuna target there had been an increasing build-up of cloud. From the 'Mandrel' screen Thorne had increased height to 14,000ft whilst Main Force had gone higher to 17,000ft. Visibility was good at those heights but the ground was completely obscured by 10/10ths stratus cloud, the tops of which could not have been more than 4,000ft high. D-Dog's time over the target was 23.52hrs. Gray came through to Thorne at 23.40hrs to say that they were running exactly to time. Reg had been scratching around his bombing equipment since they made the last change of course south of Kassel. He reported everything working. Then came Jock's voice over the intercom: 'Combat behind us. Starboard. Some distance away. Firing now stopped. I'm watching out.' There was no further report from Jock, but there was a burst of activity from the ground defences. The clouds below were suddenly illuminated by searchlights which had the effect of turning them into a vast white carpet stretching

ahead and over an area which much have included the target itself. Almost simultaneously came heavy flak in a barrage which burst in yellow-white flashes, fortunately well below the bombers. The searchlights had helped confirm that there was no hope of the target being visible and it was no surprise when the MB broadcast a 'Wanganui' attack order.

At 23.45hrs the Master Bomber made his first call to his Deputy: 'I think we'll have to call for "Wanganui". There are no signs of a break in the clouds.' The DMB replied: 'I agree. I'll wait for you to contact.' All in D-Dog were ready when the first Mosquito's target indicators hit the ground, causing a green suffused glow beneath the cloud. A minute later a 'Wanganui' flare exploded into red and green stars which hung above the cloud. As the MB's voice came over: 'Aim at the red and green flares', D-Dog's bomb doors were opened and Reg and Thorne went into their double act on the run-up to the target. The barrage from the ground had not abated but the flak was still well below the Lancasters in the Main Force shedding their bomb loads from around 17,000ft and, inexplicably, it did not even reach the

PFF aircraft at their lower heights. Reg called: 'Bombs gone!' at the end of a steady run-up to the flares, which were being held in a tightly formed concentration above the clouds as the sky target was continuously replenished by the 'Wanganui' force. A red glow from the first of the bombs exploding on the ground was shining through the clouds below as Thorne swung D-Dog on to a southerly heading 30sec after Reg had released D-Dog's load. That was giving sufficient time after 'bombs gone' for the photo-flash to operate, although it was unlikely to result in a picture of the target, or anything else apart from cloud.

From his position in the rear turret Ken had a grandstand view of the target area as they flew away from it. He reported that the red glow was becoming more intense as the Main Force aircraft poured in behind them, indicating that the attack, like the 'Wanganui' flares, was well concentrated. A particularly big explosion throwing a column of black smoke up through the cloud layer at 2-3,000ft seemed to confirm also that the Pathfinders' 'Wanganui' marking technique was once again proving effective in such conditions.

Fifteen minutes after leaving the target Gray gave Thorne a new course heading of 105° to be followed by another change which would point them in a southwesterly direction and take them south of Frankfurt. But after 120 miles on that course there was another change, this time to the northwest with Frankfurt then on the port side. On those dog-legs from Leuna there had been sporadic bursts of heavy flak on both sides of the route although, strangely, nothing within miles of the returning Lancasters. It was very cold, especially for the gunners, so cold in fact that Ernie had the aircraft's heating going full blast without roasting himself in his W/Op's compartment. The dog-legging took another turn, this time on a course to the southwest and crossing the Rhine south of Cologne. It continued for 150 miles when a turn to the northwest put them on a heading west of Brussels to cross the Belgian coast at Ostend and on across the North Sea to Orfordness. It had been a long trip with the many changes of course and constantly varying winds demanding maximum concentration and expertise from the navigators. As soon as Boris told Ernie and the rest of the crew that they were about to cross the English coast, they were not sorry to hear Ernie call base to announce their position. Boris could see it on his H2S screen, but that was the only way it could be identified because the mainland was covered by thick fog. It looked like they would be landing on FIDO, but that didn't worry them. But what did cause alarm and despondency was the reply from base directing them to land at Ford, callsign 'Coachride', an airfield some 150 miles way down south. It must be said that the reaction of the crew was remarkably restrained because, as they later admitted they were too damned tired to vent their feelings on the subject. They

were unanimous in their guesses that the fog extended northwards, the FIDO airfields had been filled with many of the 500 or so aircraft returning from Phase 1 of the night's operations, and the more southerly parts of England were presumably less affected by the fog. It transpired that they were correct in all those assumptions. Ernie passed on to the navigators details of the route to be taken to Ford as he had received them from base. Thorne swung D-Dog on to the appropriate southerly course and his first question was to Harry: 'What's the fuel situation?' Harry replied: 'If we can land pretty smartly we'll be OK, but there won't be much to spare.' Thorne asked if there was any coffee left and Reg's head and shoulders appeared below with his hand clutching a flask containing half a cup full, and still hot. No one knew much, if anything, about Ford airfield although Gray could say that the course provided by base ended about three miles from Arundel in West Sussex. As they flew south the fog diminished and after crossing the River Thames, Thorne could see searchlights and beacons ahead. They were then at 5,000ft so he commenced reducing height. Navigation lights became visible on other aircraft and by the time he radioed 'Coachride from Cutout, approaching for landing, height now 3,000ft', the sky seemed full of aircraft approaching or orbiting like bees round a honey-pot. There was no reply, so he repeated the call. Then back came:
'Cutout from Coachride. Orbit at 3,000ft and await further instructions, please.' Thorne replied:
'Message received but we are short on fuel. Can you expedite, please?' He waited and was about to repeat when the controller's voice came again:
'Reduce height to 2,000ft in a wide orbit. We will call as soon as possible'. Thorne did as he was told, making a wide orbit of the airfield to reduce interfering with aircraft doing a normal orbit, and reduced engine revs and airspeed so that D-Dog would conserve fuel and maintain height

pending further instructions from the controller. Eventually they landed to find an airfield packed with parked aircraft and others taxi-ing around the perimeter until they found a place to rest. And there was an unaccountable number of aircraft still orbiting anxiously above.

Next morning, at the crack of dawn, the crew rolled off their beds which had been found for them, and many others among the diverted crews, by kindly airmen and airwomen, and after some difficulty — they had only a hazy idea of where they had parked D-Dog — they managed to find a bowser and crew with enough fuel to get them home to Downham Market. They had not come across the other five No 635 Squadron crews in the general melee at Ford, but eventually they had all returned to Downham by midday.

Subsequent photographic reconnaissance revealed that the night's operations had been an unqualified success. The two separate attacks on the Leuna oil plants had resulted in heavy damage to almost every important installation and it seemed reasonable is assume that production had been brought to a halt. The planning of the operation, with the inspired use of available countermeasures, had caused such confusion among the enemy's raid-tracking and fighter control organisations that only 15 out of the total of 1,215 aircraft employed failed to return — 10 from the Leuna attacks, two from Berlin, and one each from Grevenbroich, Dulmen, and the 'Sweepstake' diversions.

Below:
Pölitz synthetic oil plant reduced to a smouldering wreck.

6
Daylight Over Nuremburg

There were certain areas in Germany the very names of which Bomber Command crews would rather not hear, especially when they were revealed as their targets at briefings. Essen, Cologne, Berlin, Gelsenkirchen, Hamburg, Leipzig, Munich — they all just sounded heavy and sinister. And then there was Nuremburg, a grimly threatening name even before the night of 30 March 1944 when Bomber Command lost 95 aircraft, excluding 10 which crashed on landing. Casualties among the aircrew were more than in any single operation during the war. The only good that came out of the fiasco was that it ended any ideas the planners had that a direct approach to a target would be more effective than keeping the enemy's ground and air defences guessing where the targets would be for as long as possible. The raids on Leuna, described in the previous chapter, were confirmation of the effectiveness of suitably planned dog-legs and other feints which continued to be employed on operations until victory was achieved.

After 41 operations with No 635 Squadron the Thorne crew was 'promoted' to the role of Deputy Master Bomber in a night attack on Dessau in northern Germany. Then came their first as Master Bomber in a daylight raid on the industrial complex at Dorsten in the northern part of 'Happy Valley'. They returned with, according to

the groundcrew, 40 flak holes in D-Dog. Whilst orbiting the target after dropping their 8,000lb load of TIs and bombs a piece of flak must have hit the tail plane, locking the fore and aft controls so that D-Dog went into a shallow dive. After what seemed an eternity of pushing and pulling on the control column — although it may not have been for more than a minute — Thorne heaved a sigh of relief when the column miraculously became movable and normal control was resumed. Only Harry, sitting next to Thorne, knew what had been going on and nothing was said to the others in the crew until they were back in the briefing room.

With the advances of the Allied armies after D-Day, Bomber Command extended its activities to include daylight operations on a rapidly increasing scale. The American air forces had proved it could be done, albeit often with very heavy losses, and the RAF crews were quick to respond and cope with the new conditions. During the last 10 months of the war the number of

Bomber Command daylight operations was approximately the same as those which took place at night.

On 4 March, Wg Cdr 'Tubby' Baker DSO, DFC, completed his time as squadron CO. He had always said he would not go until he had 100 operations under his hat, and in his logbook, and he achieved that number a few days before his farewell party in the Mess. He was a pilot *par excellence* and his concentration on the things that matter, and to hell with trivia, earned him the admiration of all who served with him. After the war he married Freda who had been a WAAF officer on the squadron. On leaving Downham Market, 'Tubby' had been posted to Italy but soon after his arrival he was very severely injured in a Jeep, of all things, and told he would never fly again. But he did, and became CO of No 138 Squadron on Lincolns and later on Valiants. He crowned his career in 1978 when he led the British team of four Vulcan crews from Scampton and Waddington in the annual Strategic Air Command bombing competition 'Giant Voice' in California. His place at No 635 Squadron was taken by Wg Cdr James Fordham who remained until the war ended after which he became a senior captain in BOAC.

On the evening of 10 April a battle order was posted for a daylight operation on the

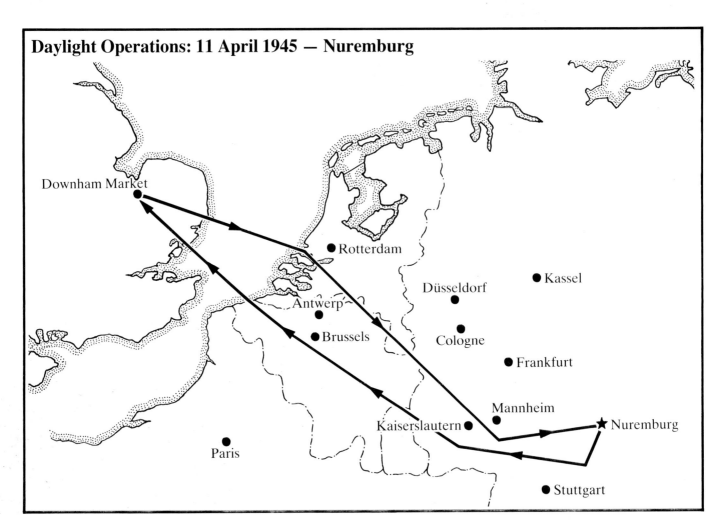

Daylight Operations: 11 April 1945 — Nuremburg

following day. Briefing was at 11.30hrs and two No 635 Squadron crews were named: those of Flt Lt Thorne and that of Sqn Ldr Hitchcock, as MB and DMB respectively. The briefing was opened as always with the removal of the curtain covering the route and target, and that day it was to be Nuremburg. Neither Thorne nor Hitchcock had experienced the doubtful pleasure of visiting in daylight that 'Holy City of Nazi creed' as someone at Bomber Command had once described it. But there had to be a first time and on that day they would be accompanied by 129 Halifaxes from the Yorkshire-based No 4 Group and 12 PFF Lancasters.

The specific targets were the railway marshalling yards with their large quantities of rolling stock and supplies massed in that area. The weather was forecast to be clear with good visibility over the route and target. A second force of 100 Halifaxes led by 14 PFF Lancasters and eight Mosquitoes would make a second stream flying 10 miles apart from the Nuremburg force. When they reached the Dutch islands they were to turn southeast towards Kaiserslautern, near Mannheim, at which point the second force would branch off east by

north to Bayreuth where a similar attack would be made on the rail marshalling yards and rolling stock. So it was the old route to Orfordness then to Jim's 'beckoning fingers', and a half-turn southeast to Kaiserslautern with Nuremburg just over 100 miles ahead after a 40° turn to port. There had been no enemy opposition of any kind until the last change of course had been made, at which point a voice came over the intercom from the bomb-aimer's compartment. It was not the voice of Reg Keary because he had finished his operational tour at the end of January when he was commissioned as pilot officer and posted to Lichfield as an instructor. His place had been taken by Flg Off Joe Clack, a bomb aimer and gunner with bags of experience and a temperament which fitted in perfectly with the sometimes unorthodox methods of the Thorne crew. 'I can see flak way ahead. Can anyone else?' They certainly had. Jock had his finger on his intercom switch to say the same thing, and Jack and Harry were making signs to each other and pointing to the black blobs in the sky which were rapidly coming closer and thicker on their track. D-Dog ploughed through it at 14,000ft with the Deputy just ahead and PFF Supporters on each side followed by the Main Force of Halifaxes streaming behind.
'Bang on time. Can you see the Deputy?' Gray announced.
Thorne replied in the affirmative and at 14.47hrs he called his Deputy: 'Portland 1 to Portland 2. Are you all set?'

Portland 2: 'All ready and about to start my run-in.' (Master Bombers had their own individual call-sign to be used on all their MB trips.)
At 15.00hrs the DMB called 'Markers gone!' Starting his run-up, Thorne could see that red TIs had fallen on either side of, and very close to, the aiming point which was easily identifiable. In fact, the whole of Nuremburg, its streets, railways and buildings lay clear beneath them.

Prominent on the port side was the famous stadium, venue of the prewar Olympics at which Hitler refused to meet the American winner of the sprint final. Over the last 70-80 miles D-Dog, and undoubtedly the other aircraft also, had been harried with frequent bumps from the exploding flak but no aircraft had been seen to go down. Then luck deserted D-Dog. Joe had just commenced his bombing run instructions to Thorne when there was a bang as the aircraft staggered from a particularly near miss, the control column started shaking and he had to force the wheel hard to starboard to rectify a violent roll to port. The target was coming up fast in Joe's bombsights, but with

109

Below:
It was the old route to Ordfordness, then to Jim's 'beckoning fingers'. *Via R. C. Sturtivant*
Left:

Bottom:
At 15.00hrs the DMB called 'Markers gone!'.

At 15.00hrs the DMB called 'Markers gone!'.

Bottom:

SOUND AND FURY. A typical daytime view of a bombing operation. Politz after a massed bombing attack – 'carpet bombing' in extremis . . .

Bottom right:

ONE OF OUR AIRCRAFT IS MISSING – a common announcement on BBC radio most evenings, exemplified here by the 'death' of Lancaster PD336 of No 90 Squadron over Wesel on 19 February 1945 as its 10,000lb high explosive bomb load detonates after a direct hit from German flak. *Crown Copyright*

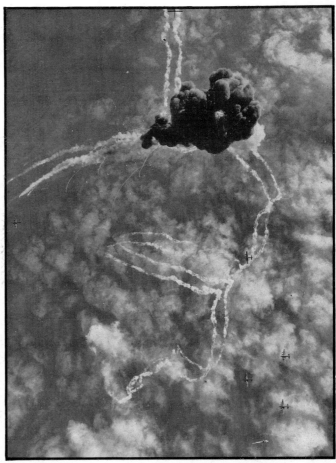

Left:
Alex Thorne's bomb load going down and hitting their target, Nuremburg, 11 April 1945. *Author*

a quick interjection of 'Bloody 'ell!' he continued his commentary. Thorne throttled back the port engines to lighten the strain and bring the port wing back to near normal in order to resume the run to the target, if it were possible in the seconds remaining. Joe called to keep it like this: 'I'll tell you when to turn on track if it's not too late . . . left . . . left . . . LEFT. Bombs gone!'

D-Dog gave a momentary shake as was usual with the sudden lessening of weight and Thorne concentrated on keeping a straight course hoping fervently that their markers and bombs would be reasonably on target. Their continuation on-course after bombs gone and the bomb doors closed was the longest 30sec the crew had experienced. D-Dog was still straining to drop the port wing so Thorne lessened the pressure necessary to keep the starboard wing down and the aircraft turned rather reluctantly to port. As he turned into a position to see the target it eased his mind to see that the red markers were all in a tight bunch and in the right place. He called Main Force and told them to bomb the red TIs. D-Dog's height had reduced to 12,000ft which enabled an orbit of the target to be carried out beneath the still oncoming Halifaxes. They were doing very well in their aiming despite the persistent flak. After two further broadcasts of 'bomb the reds' the target became obscured by smoke so it was natural that the next broadcast was 'bomb the centre of the smoke'. Exactly 9min after the first markers were dropped and Thorne was on his third orbit, the last Halifax turned for home. Thorne called the DMB: 'Hope you are OK. It seems to have gone well. Have a good trip back.' The reply came: 'Yes indeed. See you on return. Cheers.'

A quick look along the wings during the orbits had revealed the port aileron jammed in the 'up' position so it became a matter of maintaining a reduction in engine revs on that side and the speed kept down to around 140mph. The big worry was whether the vibration through the pilot's control column was caused by the damage to the aileron, or had another component also been affected by the flak hit — or hits? Happily, Harry could confirm that the fuel tanks and equipment were OK so they pressed on for home with D-Dog flying along like an injured duck. With the reduction in speed the other aircraft were soon out of sight and it was a lonely feeling to find themselves alone but thankful for the fact that the ground defences seemed to have given up; there had been no threat from enemy aircraft. And it would not be too long before they were over friendly territory. Even before they had reached the Belgian border, Jim came on the intercom: 'I don't want to worry you but two fighter aircraft are coming up fast

behind us.' That's all we need, thought Thorne, but he was immediately reassured when Jim proclaimed: 'It's OK. I can see now they are Mustangs.' In no time at all the two had formated one on each side of D-Dog. Harry jumped up and down with glee as he drew Thorne's attention to the one on the starboard side. Thorne looked across: there indeed was a Mustang, the coloured pilot of which was waving a friendly hand and sticking out from his lips and clenched between his teeth was a large cigar. They remained in formation for a while and then, with a waggle of their wings, they were away and soon out of sight. Almost immediately — it could almost have been rehearsed — the Mustangs were replaced by a Spitfire whose pilot was not smoking a cigar, but

who gave the thumbs up sign and stayed with them until they crossed into friendly territory. Harry had the happy thought to make a note of the identity code on the Spitfire's fuselage. Norman Page, No 635 Squadron's adjutant, found out the Spitfire's squadron and home base and Thorne sent a note to the pilot thanking him for his presence that afternoon. He received a reply: 'Many thanks for your letter. I could see we were in some sort of trouble. Glad you returned safely. It was a case of "do unto others . . ." Best wishes.'

The official reports following the operation noted that heavy damage had been inflicted on the sidings, goods and stores depots, leaving some 70% unserviceable. Wagon repair shops had been partially wrecked and all lines to the east were cut.

The results of enemy action: PA226 of No 429 Squadron displays the ravages of flack damage, while DV305 of No 550 Squadron suffered two fatalities amongst its crew after a fighter attack.

TOP DOG. Lancaster ED888, 'M2' of No 103 Squadron which achieved the Bomber Command record of completing 140 operational sorties. Seen here after its final sortie with its crew (left to right): Sgt Sam Cook (R/AG); Sgt George Wildeney (F/E); Flt Sgt John C. T. Tear (Nav); Flt Lt John Barnes (Pilot); Flt Sgt Derick Ireland (W/Op); Flt Sgt Michael Haslam (B/A); Sgt Arthur Clark (MU/AG). Depite its prominence it was scrapped in January 1947. *Flt Lt J. Barnes*

Above left:
ME746, 'R2' of No 166 Squadron, Kirmington,
flew 116 operations in all. Here the aircrew
present a giant DSO award to their Erks for
'Distinguished Service'. *IWM CH17997*

Left:
BIII, EE139, 'B-Baker' of No 550 Squadron,
named *Phantom of The Ruhr,* **which**
completed 121 sorties and was struck off RAF
charge on 12 January 1946.

Above:
ED611, *Uncle Joe* **of No 463 Squadron RAAF,**
Waddington with a bomb log recording 100
ops, though beneath the drawing of Joseph
Stalin is chalked '104 Not Out'. *L. Cottroll*

Right:
W4964, WS-J, of No 9 Squadron with its
cartoon of the famous whisky advertising
figure 'Johnnie Walker', which completed 106
sorties before being relegated as an
instructional airframe, 4922M.

VETERAN. ED588, VN-G, of No 50 Squadron which completed 128 ops – 118 of these with No 50 – before failing to return on 29/30 August 1944.

Lancaster R5868 remains the only genuine wartime operational PFF bomber now in existence. Now resident in the RAF Bomber Command Museum, Hendon, it actually completed 135 operational sorties, serving first with No 83 Squadron, then No 467 Squadron RAAF. During its career it carried three different insignia. The first *(above left)* was a red devil thumbing its nose above the motto *Devils of the Air,* seen here at Wyton in May 1943 with Flg Off 'Rick' Garvey (later DSO, DFC) as captain. On moving to No 467 Squadron the former OL-Q, *Queenie* became recoded as PO-S, 'Sugar' and received a fresh insignia of a nude lady kneeling, holding a bomb *(left)*, seen here with the first crew to fly R5868 with No 467 Squadron, Flg Off N. McClelland as skipper. By March 1945 'Sugar' was wearing a full bomb log of 137 operations (incorrectly), plus a quote from a boastful speech by the Luftwaffe's supremo, Hermann Göring *(right)* with one of its crews, skippered by Flg Off Bob Swift.

ED860, QR-N, 'Nan' of No 61 Squadron, seen here having its 100th op added to its bomb log, went on to complete 130 sorties before being struck off RAF charge on 29 October 1944 at Skellingthorpe. *IWM CH13454*

Right:
The nose section of DV372, PO-F of
No 467 Squadron RAAF is preserved in the
Imperial War Museum, London. It completed
49 ops between November 1943 and October
1944, then moved to No 1651 CU and was
wrecked on 4 October 1945. *IWM MH10455*

Below:
Wg Cdr Campbell Hopcroft DFC and his No 57
Squadron crew pose in front of 'Frederick II' —
this cartoon appearing on three successive
Lancs flown by Hopcroft; the third being
ED989, DX-F, 'Frederick III', which failed to
return from a sortie on 18 August 1943.
IWM CH8907

7
As the Years have Passed

Two days after the daylight raid on Nuremburg the Thorne crew were the Master Bombers on a night operation on the German naval base at Kiel. Five days later they led the second wave of bombers, part of a total of 1,000 aircraft, on a daylight raid on the naval installations at Heligoland.

On 24 April the crew went on leave, returning in time to celebrate VE-Day on the squadron – all, that is, except one. Thorne was spending a miserable two weeks at home with chickenpox! By the time he returned all the others in the crew had been posted away to places near and far.

The war was still on in the Far East, and **Boris Bressloff** had been flown out to Bangalore where he was installed as Commander, RAF Movements, until his demob in October 1946. He then joined an international group of volunteers forming Israel's embryonic air force. He flew on 20 operations as navigator on a squadron which, in his words, consisted of elderly B-17s that had been purchased from a scrap dealer. Two years later, back in the UK, he returned to hairdressing in London. He is now retired, married with two sons – one a solicitor, the other a chartered surveyor – and he and his wife Nita live in Stanmore, Middlesex.

In an earlier chapter it was explained how **Harry Parker** had flown for two years after the war as flight engineer/navigator with Gp Capt Leonard Cheshire VC during the time he was establishing his Cheshire Homes in various parts of the world. In 1949 Harry returned to his prewar job in industry, retiring from his position as engineer-in-charge of an electronics group in 1988. He is married, with one son, and he and his wife Eileen live in the West Country.

Ernie Patterson finished his RAF career as chief of flying control at Korangi Creek, near Karachi. On his return to the UK after 12 months he was greeted by his wife Kay, and their seven-month-old son. Ernie returned to his prewar job in the building trade and for 23 years until his retirement in 1988 he had his own business. He is now a widower, but he still lives in a bungalow he built for the three of them, in Darlington, Co Durham.

Reg Keary was 21 years old when he

The author, Flt Lt Alex Thorne DSO, DFC, wearing the prized PFF eagle badge of a 'qualified' Pathfinder.

joined the RAF. He did so, he explains, because he could not bear the thought of having to suffer the awful discomforts of trench warfare if he volunteered for the Army. He does not go on to say that during his first 24 Bomber Command operations he had seen two of his crew killed, two wounded, and that he had survived three subsequent emergency crash landings. After completing a total of 50 operations (the last 26 of them with the Thorne crew) Reg was commissioned as a pilot officer and posted to Singapore as RAF Embarkation Officer. Demobbed in 1946 he began to look for a job. He replied to an advertisement in the *Daily Telegraph* stating: 'Large London bank requires staff' and received a reply from the Westminster (now NatWest) Bank. He joined them and was thankful to reach the humble rank of Chief Cashier! Reg has remained a bachelor and lives in Essex.

When **Jim Raymont** was demobbed he went back to his old job as a technician in an old-established firm of jewellers in Birmingham. He retired some 20 years later to enjoy life at home with his wife, and step-son and step-daughter who lived near them. Sadly, Jim is now a widower and lives alone, but he is very active in his 85th year and keeps in contact with all of the old crew.

The war over, **Graham Rose** did not waste any time in taking steps to realise the ambition he had often talked about. Not surprisingly, he was welcomed at Reading University where he gained a degree in geology. His wife Jean, whom he had married soon after leaving the RAF, says he was packing his belongings after the degree awards ceremony when the senior lecturer put his head around the door of Gray's room and said: 'If you'd like to stay here as lecturer you could stop your packing'. Needless to say, that is just what he did, ultimately to become senior lecturer himself. Some years after he retired, Gray was at home writing Christmas cards when he had a heart attack and died. There could not have been a better and more self-effacing member of a bomber crew than Gray. So far as is known he is the only member of the Thorne crew no longer with us but there are three who cannot be traced.

Jock Scott who was ever present as mid-upper gunner, **Don Suttie** and **Joe Clack,** wireless operator and bomb aimer respectively on many of the crew's operations, left the squadron vowing to keep in touch, but efforts to contact them so far have been unsuccessful. If any one of them should read this, Thorne hopes they will write to him care of the publishers of this book.

As for Thorne, when he returned to Downham Market three weeks after VE-Day he found that No 635 Squadron had virtually ceased to exist, and an air of anti-climax pervaded throughout the station. The majority of the aircrews had already dispersed in the manner of his own crew, and Lancasters were being taken from their dispersal points and flown away to finish their lives in various ways, mostly on RAF Maintenance Units. The Messes were sparsely populated and among those who used them the main topics of

conversation were centred upon the possibilities of when, and to where, the next batch of postings would determine their future until their demob dates. There were some odd periods of activity to relieve the monotony. Scratch crews were organised to fly ground personnel over Germany to show them the results of the bomber offensive on targets which had been just place names to them. Lancasters were also used to take food and other necessities to be dropped over areas on the Continent that were suffering from the immediate aftermath of war, and flights were made to Italy to bring troops back to the UK. Thorne was one who gathered a crew for that purpose: the take-off from Bari airfield in Italy with 30 soldiers and their kit spread throughout the fuselage provided some of the diciest moments of his flying career.

At last, in September 1945, three months before he was due to be demobbed, he was told that the CO of RAF Wyton, the wartime operational HQ of the Pathfinder Force situated 30 miles southwest of Downham Market, was looking for someone to write the history of Wyton airfield. It was suggested that 'it would be something for him to do' so he made what he thought would be one last visit to D-Dog's dispersal and off he went. But he was back again for one day at the end of September after a phone call from one of the old groundcrew to tell him that D-Dog was to be flown away the following day. It was a miserable morning with drizzling rain when an engineer and pilot arrived to take D-Dog away to No 15 Maintenance Unit at Wroughton, near Swindon. He looked as majestic as always. The remaining mem-

Above:
Thorne pictured at Elmdon Airfield, near Birmingham in 1943 where he spent 18 months as a flying instructor before joining the PFF. *Author*

bers of the groundcrew and Thorne watched him being started up, taxy round the runway to take-off, and with a familiar roar from his engines finally disappear into the low cloud. Nineteen years later Thorne heard that D-Dog had shared the same fate as so many of his contemporaries. He had been broken up for scrap in May 1947.

Soon after Thorne had collected his civilian suit, not forgetting a trilby hat, he was appointed secretary and manager of the newly opened Pathfinder Association and Club in Mount Street, London. One of its purposes was to assist ex-Pathfinders to find suitable jobs on their return to civilian life, a task in which it proved eminently successful. The Club side of the enterprise also prospered and it was often referred to in the press as 'one of London's famous Clubs'. Thorne retired in 1955 to become director of a public relations company and, for 10 years, editor of *Air Mail*, the magazine of the Royal Air Force Association. He lives in Surrey with his wife Madeleine.

Honours

In October 1946, RAF Downham Market ceased to exist when the airfield and surrounding countryside returned to the comparative tranquility of their prewar agricultural roles. The perimeter tracks still exist and there is evidence in many parts of the lanes, and woods, of the

buildings that saw so much activity during the war years. The huts which were the crews' billets in the orchard of the ancient village church have long since gone, but the typically Norfolk house on the opposite side of the lane which was the station commander's residence still retains the rural attractiveness of a Constable painting.

Downham Market was a bomber station for little more than two years. But if honours count for anything, the records of its aircrews during the period must rank among the great. They included two VCs: Flt Sgt Arthur Aaron of No 218 Squadron, and Sqn Ldr Ian Bazalgette of No 635 Squadron. Members of the latter squadron alone, in its short life of 20 months, were awarded 14 DSOs and more than 100 DFCs and DFMs. They included all the officers and NCOs who flew in the Thorne crew.

Above right:
Postwar reunion: Members of the PFF Association, including Thorne, meet General Adolf Galland and other former Luftwaffe fighter pilots at Heathrow airport. *Author*

Right:
A recent picture of the Thorne crew — Left to right: Ernest Patterson (wireless operator), Jim Raymont (rear gunner), Alex Thorne, Boris Bressloff (radar navigator), Harry Parker (flight engineer), Reg Keary (bomb aimer), with Mrs Nita Bressloff. *Author*

ROYAL AIR FORCE
BOMBER COMMAND
1939 – 1945

SOME OF THE MEN WHO FLEW
IN LANCASTERS